Shift

·······

*New Paradigms for a
New Earth*

HEATHER WALLACE

TURNING
STONE
PRESS

First published in 2013 by Turning Stone Press, an
imprint of Red Wheel/Weiser, LLC
With offices at:
665 Third Street, Suite 400
San Francisco, CA 94107
www.redwheelweiser.com

Copyright © 2013 by Heather Wallace
All rights reserved. No part of this publication may be
reproduced or transmitted in any form or by any means,
electronic or mechanical, including photocopying, recording,
or by any information storage and retrieval system, without
permission in writing from Red Wheel/Weiser, LLC.
Reviewers may quote brief passages.

ISBN: 978-1-61852-064-7

Cover design by Jim Warner
Cover image: © ixpert / Shutterstock

Printed in the United States of America

10 9 8 7 6 5 4 3 2 1

For Holly.
In deepest gratitude.

Contents

	Acknowledgments	vii
	Preface	ix
1	The Earth School	1
2	A New Earth	7
3	From Head-Centered to Heart-Centered: The New Operating System	15
4	Becoming Mindful of Your Creative Energy Contribution	19
5	The Earth Curriculum	27
6	The Law of Attraction and Manifestation	47
7	Conscious, Subconscious, and Consciousness	57
8	Your Multidimensionality	69
9	Reincarnation and the Nature of Time	77
10	Free Will versus Predetermination	85
11	Personal Responsibility and Healthy Conflict Resolution	89
12	The Emotional, Mental, and Spiritual Selves: Healing and Integration	97
13	The Shift into a New Vibrational Range of Experience	113
14	Psychic Abilities and Your Inner Navigation System	127
15	Divine Timing	137

16	The Role of Faith in the Creative Process	143
17	How to Create Your Reality and Your Role as Co-Creator	151
18	The People-Pleasing Epidemic and its Antidote: Self-Love	169
19	Conclusion: Parting Words	193
	About the Author	195

Acknowledgments

As always, I'd like to thank those who have supported and loved me throughout all the endeavors of my life. My family—those who have been my solid, unwavering system of love and support always. A tremendous and heartfelt thank you to my friends on the other side. My guides, guardian angels, and other teachers. I am so incredibly blessed for the wisdom, guidance, love, and support you have given me. Thank you for showing me what is beyond the physical realm and for teaching me about love and personal freedom at a deeper level.

Preface

I began channeling in 2003 when a book literally fell off a bookstore shelf at my feet and I was strongly guided to turn to a particular page—which was titled "automatic writing." The "other side" sure knows how to get our attention when they want it! Previous to this I had experienced encounters with those on the other side (or the spirit plane). I am what one might call clairvoyant or clairaudient, although I still find those terms uncomfortable. It is difficult to put labels on the ways I receive information from the other side. I am a *translator*; that is the term I find most accurate and that I am most comfortable with using.

Being sensitive and having the ability to translate for those in other planes of existence, the notion of automatic writing, or channeling, seemed like a natural progression in my life's journey when the book dropped off the shelf at my feet and first introduced me to the term "automatic writing." People most often ask who I am translating for when I write and how I know it's not somebody who is harmful. Both are valid, excellent questions. The easier question to answer is the latter. I never speak with anyone who is not in my greatest good. I connect only with those who are working for the greater good of all and who are working from love and integrity. I have protection in place to prevent anyone else from communicating with me. Yes, sometimes they show up, but my protective barriers prevent any communication unless I initiate it. I don't!

For the purposes of writing a book, I partner with those who are at a level that we would call "enlightened." These are ones who are at a teacher or guide level, who are not incarnating as we are because they have already mastered those lessons. For this particular book, I partnered with beings from the Pleiadian star system. These are beings who are "spiritually aware" or "advanced" in our terms and have often made contact with us in an effort to assist us in our expansion. They are benevolent, loving, supportive, and kind. It was an honor to connect with "Holly," the representative of the group I worked with for this book. I always ask for a name when collaborating with one of these teachers on the other side because it is far easier for me to have a reference during this period of collaboration. Thankfully, I am given easy names, as in this case—Holly. I seriously doubt that Holly is this being's true name. I don't even know if they have names at all where they live. But for the sake of our working together, she chose to be called Holly. I appreciate that my teachers do this and keep it simple. They are not worried about labels and I think they pick something that they find jazzy and fun (I have also worked with "Primrose," "Gigi," and "Boots"). I truly appreciate the "down to earth" (no pun intended) aspect of this name picking—not identifying themselves as Bxilator or Volpheneus or something of that sort!

So, for this particular book I translated for Holly, who is Pleiadian. This was my first collaboration with anyone from the Pleiades and I did not see it coming. I am used to working with those on the other side, or the spirit plane, and was not expecting someone from another star system to show up. Immediately I was impressed with Holly's energy which is so kind, loving, and reverent for the human race and our journey. Throughout the book her tone is respectful and kind. Never is there chastising or judgment for the way we live or for our confusion about who we are. I was humbled beyond humbled and honored beyond honored to receive communication from Holly. She is beautiful.

The intention of this book is to help us see where we are perhaps stuck in certain "programs" that aren't serving us and how to come more into alignment with our authentic self. Holly presents powerful, paradigm-shifting information about why we are here, what it's all about, and the nature of our connection to Source. Holly lovingly points out things we have likely been doing for years without even realizing it—things that prevent us from truly embracing our divinity. Examples of this are our systems for labeling and categorizing one another (and ourselves), conflict between our mental and emotional selves, and seeking a sense of worth from external factors such as the love and approval of others.

I found it incredibly beneficial and useful that Holly talks of our creative energy and how that contributes to both our personal quality of life and global cohesiveness. Even for those who have long been aware that we are creating with our thoughts, feelings, beliefs, and actions, Holly presents information about this that will provide deeper insight and surely some "a-has!" about this process and about ourselves. It takes the reader with knowledge and experience of his or her creative power to a deeper level of understanding. Likewise, it presents to the novice the necessary information to become aware of and to begin *consciously* using their creative potential.

This book was kept intentionally short. There is a lot to chew on in the information presented here. This is life-changing information that is intended to be absorbed at a deep level of being. The longer the book, the more information presented, and thus more is lost as one tries to process many deep spiritual truths. This is a little handbook full of big wisdom. It can be likened to a roadmap to joy, freedom, and love.

Simply reading the map won't get you there, though; you have to get behind the wheel and drive. The information is here to change your life in a powerful and joyful way, but like any information, it is yours to do with as you wish. It is my sincerest and deepest pleasure to share this book with you. I have the unique pleasure of experiencing the love and power that comes through these words as I translate them. My hope in sharing this with you is only that it will bring you more joy, more fulfillment, and a genuine love and appreciation for your self. My goal in all endeavors is to help people realize how amazing and beautiful they are. That is why I do this and it is why I love it. I love you, and I want *you* to love you too. All of the pages following this introduction are translated and in Holly's voice, not my own.

In Love,
Heather

～ 1 ～

The Earth School

THE FIRST MATTER OF BUSINESS we need to attend to is our introduction. We would like to talk about our origins so you have a clearer sense of who we are. We are a group of beings working together to put these words on paper, through Heather, our translator. I am the "elected speaker," meaning that I am the one that is acting as the mouthpiece for the group, although this is a group effort. This is simply to minimize confusion and maximize clarity. The translation process can be tricky on its own, let alone if the translator were to have multiple beings speaking to them at once, or even switching off from one to another. It is far more efficient that this information is presented to the translator by me, and I will take on the task of representing our group.

We are a group of beings from the Pleiades star system and we have long been interested in your spiritual growth and transformation as humans. You are beautiful souls (and brave!) and we delight in working with you. There have been several channels who have connected with us and written about our culture and shared our wisdom. We are choosing to work with Heather, now, because the timing is right for our current message and she was standing at the ready to be a translator for us. This is a two-way service. Heather is acting as our translator and getting our words out there. Likewise, this is a process that greatly services her spiritual path as well.

To begin we would like to embrace the human race in our love and our gratitude. We know you look upon one another and your world at large and think, "*Oh, what a mess!*" But the work you have done as a civilization is amazing. You have truly made leaps and bounds in your spiritual progress and the growth continues at large. We stand back and applaud you all. Well done.

This kind of work that you came to do is not easy. The earth plane is a most difficult curriculum! It is not for the faint of heart. When you come into a physical lifetime from the realm of spirit, you do so with a pretty firm game plan in place. You are each walking your own unique path of learning and growth. Just as a new student at a new school shows up on the first day armed with his or her schedule of planned courses, you too show up in life with your "planned courses" of study. For some it may be Humility; for others, perhaps Relationships or Compassion. You see? You are here doing your spiritual work. You came into this lifetime with clear intentions about what you wanted to accomplish. The experiences you have and the people you meet along the way help you to accomplish those goals. And you all do this with no conscious memory of what it is you came here to do! Brave! The more aware one is of his or her lessons, the more he or she can work in harmony with those lessons. They don't feel as "punishing" when you know there is a greater purpose at play. That is not to say all your lessons are painful and feel "punishing." But this earth realm is a place where physical and emotional pain and suffering can be experienced and therefore many of your experiences can be very challenging. At the soul level, all experience is rewarding.

Let us look to the Nazi movement as an example. One may be inclined to look upon the Holocaust as atrocious, horrific, and unnecessary. Indeed, the experiences had by those who were persecuted were horrific. But the Holocaust had a larger movement behind it, one that most are not aware of because it is not obvious on its surface. The Holocaust propelled humanity into a new era of awareness. It was absolutely instrumental in waking people up—at large—to issues of intolerance and prejudice. Without such an extreme occurrence as the Holocaust, awareness would have taken far longer in coming and many more violent and destructive acts would have occurred before humanity reached the point it did through one single large-scale act as the Holocaust. As violence and destruction are an available means of learning in the earth school, they can be some of the *most efficient* ways to enact change.

Please know that life is eternal and can never truly be lost. When you leave your body you remain very much alive in spirit. So those who chose to "die" in the Holocaust bravely offered (not at the conscious level but at the soul level) to assist in propelling humanity *forward* into an awakening era of tolerance before even more extreme and disastrous events took place. What was gained in awareness through the Holocaust far outweighs what would have been lost had it not occurred.

The nature of learning in your world is such that there are many available tools through which to learn. Violence has long been a tool used by many for learning in your history. There are realms of existence where violence doesn't exist. There are other realms of existence that experience far more violence than yours. Everyone who is here—on the earth plane—is so for a reason. Nobody goes to the wrong "school." There is a much greater plan at work and truly all serves the greater plan, which is *good*.

Let's put this in context. A child who is learning to ride a bike will likely first experience several falls that result in scraped knees and hands. That will hurt and the child will cry. But are the parents outraged? No, they know that falling and scrapes are part of the process and serve the greater goal, which is a smooth ride. It is an example in the simplest form. You are all learning to ride a bike. You are each learning to ride a bike at the individual, personal level and you are also learning to ride the collective bicycle.

There are naturally going to be a lot of falls and scrapes before humanity can sit on a collective bicycle and ride smoothly in harmony. What does a parent do when the child falls and scrapes her hands? The parent kisses the scrapes and hugs the child. This is the same strategy we suggest you use when you fall off of your bike or you see others falling off of the collective bicycle. Send love to the areas that need healing. It only adds fuel to the fire to damn and curse a person or situation.

What is truly healing is love. It is the most powerful energy in the Universe. So send love to the scrapes of the world and to the scrapes in your own life. You are meant to fall off your bike—that is how you learn. When you do, send love and healing to yourself—to those parts of yourself that you do not like or are trying to change. Love dissolves the resistance that keeps struggle alive. Kiss your scrapes (love yourself no matter what) and kiss the scrapes of the world too (send love instead of anger/hate/resentment when "atrocities" are committed). Let this become your practice. This is the most powerful practice anyone can take on. It is truly what will heal your world.

≈ 2 ≈

A New Earth

THE NEW EARTH that has been emerging is at a much different vibrational resonance than before. As such, much of the previous means of learning are falling away. A higher vibration of conflict resolution is emerging. Watching this emergence from our vantage point is breathtaking. It is a remarkable and beautiful transformation that is occurring on your planet.

We have long been key players in this state of advancement on your planet. The Pleiadians and the human race have a long relationship. We have been interested in your state of affairs for some time and as benevolent beings who seek to promote the expansion of light, we have stepped in from time to time to assist you. There is no need to worry—nothing sci-fi about this! This is not an alien invasion type of thing! You have friends in other places in the Universe (us included) and friends help friends. We want nothing more than to see the evolution of the human race take you into an era of enlightenment where peace and cooperation prevails.

From a vibrational standpoint, your world is no longer at the same vibrational frequency it once was. The vibrational plane you are living in is quite different than it was prior to 2013. The rules are different now. In fact, the truly liberating thing is: There are no rules. The primary goal of this new space is for people to learn how to actively and benevolently co-create. It is a space of deeper self-awareness, where people are now learning to really ask themselves, "What do I want?" and then learning how to achieve that without the old usual baggage of should/should not, guilt, grief, feelings of worthlessness, and other self-deprecating energies. This is a space of deeper learning about action and consequence, cause and effect. You are making choices and experiencing the consequences of those choices at a new level. It is as if you have been in the third grade and now you are in the eighth grade. New lessons, new experiences, new levels of independence and responsibility are now available to you.

The vibration of the earth plane has gone up in frequency and therefore new and different forms of learning and experience are available that resonate at this new frequency. This new space is one of freedom and exploration. It is about learning to follow your heart, speak your truth, and honor the self. This is fairly new terrain for most of you. The programs that most of you were raised with are about putting others before the self, worrying about what others think, and stifling your self-expressions and truths. You are now learning to operate from a space of authentic self-love and self-expression. Naturally, as you have been raised with old programs of self-denial, all sorts of fears may arise as you move forward in speaking your truth and expressing yourself authentically. These fears may feel magnified and overwhelming and that is natural. As we said, you are now in a new vibratory space. With everything resonating at a different frequency than before, you are going to feel and process things differently. What maybe didn't ruffle you so much before might now feel like acute irritation. When people don't understand this change, they may feel like they are a basket case, like they are losing their mind and falling to pieces.

Many are experiencing feelings of anxiety, nervousness, fear, and paranoia. This is fairly typical when a shift in vibrational frequency occurs in the plane in which you are living. The emotions you are used to experiencing at a certain frequency have now been amplified, as they are now at a higher frequency. As the vibrational frequency of the plane has shifted, so has the energy of *everything*—thoughts, feelings, and actions. Everything has shifted up. So what this means is that what once did not feel like such a big deal may now feel amplified. This is why it is beneficial for you to heal the aspects of self that no longer serve who you want to be. These aspects will continue to feel amplified, causing you anxiety and nervousness until you let those energies go.

What is triggering you now are those things that you carried with you from the previous vibrational space to this new vibrational space. The vibrational frequency has shifted—you were once living within one range of frequency and now you are living in another. When this happens, those who are used to operating within one bandwidth of frequency will go through an adjustment phase and learning curve as they adapt to the new bandwidth. The shift in frequency fully occurred at the end of 2012. So from 2012 to 2013 you went into this new bandwidth of frequency. This is why there was a lot of illness at the start of 2013—a lot of people were physically adjusting to this new space. Part of this adjustment includes attuning your physical body to the new bandwidth. Anything that does not resonate at this newer vibrational frequency will come up for release. This caused, and is still causing emotional, mental, and physical upheaval and turbulence. Fears that may have felt minor before became acute.

One of the greatest tools at your disposal for healing, moving energy, and finding balance is your breath. Breathing fully and deeply will tremendously assist you right now. Try to become very conscious of your breath and notice if it is shallow. Breathe deeper—not to the point of hyperventilation, but so you get a full and complete breath of air into your body and exhale it completely as well. Breath counting is a good exercise for this. Count to three on the inhale and count to three on the exhale. Then count to four on the inhale and count to four on the exhale. Then count to five, six, and so on until you can count to seven on your inhale and count to seven on the exhale. A full breath then will take fourteen seconds: a seven-second inhale and a seven-second exhale. This is one of the most incredibly cleansing tools at your disposal. It will move stagnant energy out and pull new vibrant energy in. You can do this wherever you are—in the car, at work, at the store. You are already breathing; you may as well make it really work for you! Deep breathing is one of the core components of optional health.

We are assisting you as your earth plane goes through significant changes. These changes have been and continue to cause bizarre weather patterns and natural disasters. This type of change, on such a large scale, will inevitably result in such events. This is *planetary* evolution that is going on. Your physical planet earth, which is a living, sentient being as you are, is undergoing a massive shift in vibrational frequency. This in turn results in a massive shift in consciousness for its inhabitants. When this process of shifting began, many in the Universe sat up and took notice. It is a huge event and all events of such magnitude draw spectators. We have long seen the trajectory of this path your planet is on and we've also been aware of the possible outcomes. In that sense we have acted as friends and stepped in to assist when things were in the balance. We helped to guide things in a direction of light. You have many helpers, not just us, who care about your planet and all of its inhabitants.

Through these earth changes, humans are changing too. Many of you are now able to access information you weren't before. Many people are expanding their awareness to a new level that was not even available to you before. The range of information and awareness available to you has expanded. Some look at this and call it "waking up"; others will refer to it as "remembering." We think of it as reclaiming. Many of you are reclaiming your innate power and your intuitive abilities.

Much of your society's age-old programming is unraveling. Through this unraveling process, people begin to realize their worth and power and begin to love themselves. All of those programs that told you who you should be and how you should behave are coming under serious scrutiny. They are coming undone. So many more children are now being raised to feel with their hearts and to love one another unconditionally and most of all to love their selves unconditionally. This is the new program that is running. And this one, contrary to previous programs, is actually in accordance with your higher self. This in turn causes less of a fissure between your higher self and your personality self (your identity).

The gap between who you are and who you think you are is closing. Isn't that awesome?! The spiritual evolution taking place on your planet—and the rate at which it is happening—truly is awesome.

It is hard work, this process of evolution, and we applaud your efforts. As the earth is shifting into a new vibrational space, so must you shift in order to remain compatible to your host. This means that which does not resonate within the new vibration must go. This involves a process through which long-buried, deep-seated emotional and mental trauma and stress come to the surface. All of those things that push your buttons or trigger you are being brought up. This can make for a rocky road, with depression, anger, confusion, or irritability, just to name a few symptoms.

You may find your physical body changing, too, as you are being restructured. Slimming down is common. Bloating is common. Minor aches and pains are common. Your emotional and spiritual bodies are going through such dramatic change that it is inevitable the physical body will as well. Your physical body holds emotional stress and trauma and this energy can literally shape your body. Imagine if the emotional imbalances were released and healed. It stands to follow that your physical body would change as well, as it is no longer being influenced by those energy blocks. People may find their posture changes; they may even notice their bone structure changes. This is a massive upheaval/shifting process we are talking about here and it affects *all* levels of your being. When you go to the doctor with a belly ache he prescribes something to reduce your pain. You have all been carrying around "bellyaches" for years and now the prescription is being delivered. You are not just masking the pain this time, though, you are genuinely healing it.

Deep-seated fears and insecurities are coming to the surface and being healed. You are attuning to a different vibration than you were accustomed to before and many of the insecurities and fears you have long held do not resonate with this new vibration. They are therefore being rooted out—they can no longer exist where you are going, so to speak. Please do not be alarmed, or even mildly ruffled. This is a natural process of spiritual evolution that is occurring and has been occurring on your planet. The progress that you are making is astounding.

⇒ 3 ⇐

From Head-Centered to Heart-Centered: The New Operating System

THE PAST IS THE PAST—do not look there for future direction. The things that worked in the past are no longer the most effective means of progress. Historically, the past has been used to help determine how to proceed in the present and/or future. We are saying from here on out, wipe the slate clean. When you stand in the present moment looking ahead, trying to make decisions about which way to go or how to handle a situation, do it from a clean slate. Let go of what strategies worked in the past. There is a new energy predominating now and it affects all things, including conflict resolution and decision making. The past is no longer a reliable marker for how future decisions are made. You are moving—quite rapidly—away from an era of predominately head-centered thinking into an era of predominately heart-centered being. When such a shift as this occurs, it is no longer useful to refer to old paradigms to navigate within a time frame that is using a completely different paradigm.

This new paradigm that has been emerging requires you to *feel* rather than analyze. This is not so much about emotional versus mental, but about using your intuitive guidance system rather than your brain. Your brain has been programmed to respond in all kinds of ways that are not necessarily beneficial to you. As emotional imbalances ("baggage," as you say) have shaped your behavior—decisions, interactions, choices, perceptions, responses, and reactions—the brain has been conditioned by that behavior. Neural pathways in your brain are created (and thus create your reactionary habit patterns) based upon what neurons have continually been fired over and over again. If neural pathways have been made by continually making fear-based decisions, this will be your automatic go-to response whenever you are faced with a choice. In this way your emotions are shaping the neural patterns of your brain.

So that being said, if you are faced with a choice, which approach is more likely to net you an authentic, positive experience: your analytic approach (using a brain that may have predominately fear-based wiring) or your intuitive sense of what *feels* right? This then begs the question: Can your intuition be clouded by fear, as your mind has been?

Your actual intuition is clear, unclouded, and unbiased. What can be murky is your *interpretation* of your intuitive feelings. Think about it: You feel something intuitively, and then what happens next? The brain goes into analyzing it! So in the end you are likely acting from your mental process of analysis and not your initial intuitive guidance. This is why a lot of people, after experiencing a traumatic event, will say, "I knew better, *but* . . .", or "I had a gut feeling something wasn't right, *but* . . ."

It's where that "but" comes in that the analytic mind has taken over intuitive guidance.

You are all well equipped with this sense of intuitive guidance. Bringing your awareness to your heart center and checking in with what you *feel* is your greatest tool.

By tuning into your heart center you will begin to rewire your brain with new neural pathways. When you stop using the pathways created by fear-based decision making, they will weaken. You will then begin building and strengthening new pathways that are harmonious with your higher self. When you are in harmony spiritually, mentally, and emotionally, you live in balance. From this space, conflict resolution (both personally and globally) becomes a fairly easy and heart-centered process. This has to begin at the individual level. When enough people shift their paradigm from head-centered to heart-centered, you will in turn create a society that works from the heart. Imagine what your governments would look like then!

When decisions and choices are made from this intuitive heart-centered space, what prevails is what is in the best interest of all, not just a few. This is decision making at its most authentic and spiritual form. Heart-centered thinking is aligning with your higher self, not simply giving in to emotion. Your higher self has clarity, without all the baggage, and when you align with this part of your being, you are living an authentic expression of your true essence.

This is the shift that is happening now. This is the kind of paradigm shift that has been underway as your planet (and consequently you) shifts to a new vibration. What worked before no longer resonates at this new frequency. You cannot expect to move into a new era with outdated tools. Think of it like trying to run a farm with old rusty farm machinery from the early 1900s. Not efficient, not useful, not productive. And so, as you enter a new era on your planet, it stands to reason that you would need new tools and modes of operation. Your operating system is being upgraded.

The push toward this new paradigm of heart-centered living is a process that has been underway for some time. In order to shift from head-dominated to heart-dominated thinking, a massive upheaval of energies takes places as you completely alter and re-wire your energetic system to support this new paradigm.

Some of you may have experienced heart flutters or tingling. These are common side effects to this re-wiring process. You may also notice yourself going back and forth between how you used to respond to things to a new, more balanced way of responding to situations. You may feel shaky or nervous in situations that before did not have that effect on you. When you begin to run energy on a new wiring system it is common to feel certain physical ramifications. To maintain a good state of health it is suggested to support your body during this process of restructuring by eating high vibrational foods (lots of veggies, preferably as close to raw as possible) and whole foods without trans fats, refined sugars, and hydrogenated oils. Walking, yoga, dancing, and other forms of exercise are excellent means of moving energy in your body. Singing, chanting, and toning are also nice methods of healing and provide vibration throughout the body, both physical and energetic.

Your body will tell you what it needs, so tune in and listen to your body. It may crave a massage or a certain vitamin or mineral. Your physical body is an amazing host and deserves to be treated with all the love and care in your heart.

≈ 4 ≈

Becoming Mindful of Your Creative Energy Contribution

THE CLIMATE OF CHANGE on earth right now is creating a lot of upheaval, both globally and at the personal level, and it is common for one to view this and feel discouraged. Please know that everything is okay. The changes you see are not truly catastrophic in nature but rather a natural part of the transformation process. The nature of these changes is to rid the earth of long-held energies that no longer serve and to make room for new light to come in. It is essentially the same process that you are going through at the individual level.

Anytime a being (in this case the earth) shifts into a higher vibrational frequency, it must lose all energies in its field that do not resonate at the newer vibration. It is like a massive cleaning-out of a closet to make room for the new. The entire process is a *positive* experience. It may not look this way to you as you witness the natural disasters and the deaths and land destruction that result. When you shift your perception and view these experiences in a new light, they will no longer seem catastrophic. Remember that life is eternal; no one truly dies.

Those who lose their lives in these natural disasters have chosen to move on and return to the realm of spirit.

The soul knows what it is doing and does not leave a body unless it is ready. This knowledge the soul has of when it is "time to go" typically does not reach the conscious mind. This is partly why death seems devastating to you. It is viewed as tragic because the belief is often that the person who died was not ready to go. Both the process of coming into physical form and leaving the physical form are well planned by you at the soul level. So in actuality, nobody leaves "before their time." Your life does not begin and end when you are born into this physical body and when you leave it. Your life is a continuous journey that involves life in the spirit realm and the occasional incarnation into the physical realm. Back and forth you go, like world-class travelers.

Likewise, your planet earth is a sentient being and is going through her own process of growth and exploration. When a purging of her energies takes place, it is a natural process of growth. It is okay to feel sad or feel compassion when you see these events occur. We are not telling you that you should not feel anything. We are simply trying to help you *understand* the situation as it really is, so that your feelings are in harmony with what is really going on. People experience all kinds of emotions when they do not understand something. When you accurately understand a situation, you may still have feelings about it, but your emotions will stem from an accurate understanding of what is going on. This is a more balanced way to respond to a situation.

Recall what we said previously about sending love to those people and situations that need healing (kissing the scrapes)? The same applies here. When you hear of an earthquake, or tsunami, or hurricane, or any other event in which destruction occurs and lives are lost, send love. Send healing love to the earth and to all those involved. This approach is incredibly healing. We understand that you mean well when you express emotions of outrage, anger, and pity in these situations, but the energy of these emotions is not healing. Love and compassion are healing energies and go a long way in healing a situation. This is an important subject, so let's spend some time with it.

Your emotions are creative energy and have a creative effect on the outer world. If you are hoping to create particular results, let's say peace, then it will be necessary for you to align your emotions so that they are an energetic match to peace. Anger and fear do not create peace. History has shown you this. Love and tolerance *do* support peace. You can think of this in terms of physics. Like energies attract like energies and result in creation. Since every expression of emotion you have carries its own energetic vibration, then it stands to reason that if like attracts like, your emotions need to be in sync with the vibration of peace if that is what you are trying to create.

Let's look at this on the individual level, not globally. Say you want peace in your romantic relationship with your partner. I'm sure you can feel intuitively which set of emotions will assist you in creating a peaceful reality: jealousy, rage, mistrust, lying, and envy, or love, kindness, trust, faithfulness, and appreciation. Now suppose you are generating these emotions that sync with peace, and your partner is not. Since you are co-creating your relationship reality with your partner, you will not create a genuine sense of peace and well-being in the relationship if only one person is on board. You may succeed in creating a peaceful inner reality for yourself, but for the relationship of two people to rest on a solid foundation of peacefulness, both partners must be contributing energetically to that.

It is important, then, in both your personal life and as a part in the larger community, to monitor what kind of energy you are expressing on a day-to-day basis. Do you walk through life angry, irritable, and frustrated and then get mad that life feels frustrating instead of harmonious? It is imperative that *you* take responsibility in your life for creating the kind of life you want.

A very common mistake that people unknowingly make occurs when they are watching or listening to the news. Let's use the example of Sally. Sally very much wants peace and love to prevail in the world. Sally is a peaceful and loving person and expresses these energies often as she goes about her day. Then Sally sits down to watch the news. She hears about another car bombing, a terrorist cell that is growing, a weakening economy, and any number of local shootings. Now, without realizing it, Sally is going to contribute to these situations, one way or another, by her response to them. Because Sally very much cares about peace and wishes the world would stop being such a violent place, she gets angry and disgusted at this news broadcast. She curses and directs her anger at the ones who "just aren't getting it"—the ones, she feels, who continue to contribute to the problem, making peace impossible. What Sally does not realize is that her energy is creative. By adding anger and frustration to an already inflammatory situation, she is helping to *perpetuate* exactly that which she wishes to cease!

If Sally truly wants to contribute to the healing of these situations, she needs to send healing energies to them. Anger and frustration are not healing energies.

Sending love and compassion to these situations contributes to their healing. How do you send love to a terrorist? Remove the label. Instead of labeling one as a "terrorist," think of them as a misguided child of God. *All* beings are expressions of the divine. Those who have lost their connection so profoundly that they feel it is noble to blow up cars and buildings *need* healing energy. They do not need even more energy of anger and hate! They are already running on ample supplies of those energies.

This shift in thinking and feeling may take some practice. But if it is hard work for you, then you have an indicator where *you* need some healing. Healing (love) is needed anywhere and anytime there is a withholding of love. This is a big shift in your evolution—to be able to move from anger to love. Pat yourself on the back every time you succeed. If you are faced with ten opportunities through the day to send love instead of anger to a person and/or situation and you succeed two out of those ten times, celebrate those two successes! Celebrate them and relish them and focus on those two scenarios where you expressed a loving response in order to generate more energy toward future expressions of love. Every time you have a choice and you choose love, celebrate! It is counterproductive to stew on the eight opportunities you had and did not allow love to prevail. When there is love in your life, focus there and you allow it to grow. Use the other opportunities as tools for learning. See where you could have responded differently and then let them go.

Your emotional responses to people and situations are ingrained, that is, you have likely been following an emotional response pattern for most of your life. These patterns can be largely based on fear—fear of judgment, fear of death, fear of failure, fear of loss, and so on. To learn to respond differently in situations—especially situations that trigger you—you need to become aware of *why* you are responding in the way you are. Your mind will be quick to come up with all kinds of rational justifications, so do not look there for answers. Let the mind talk if it wants to, but don't put much stock in what it has to say. To get to the bottom of this—of why you respond to certain people and/or situations with fear instead of love—you must feel your way to the answer. It's that heart-centered thinking we talked about earlier. Really tune into your self, at that deeper emotional level and see what it is that is triggering you. Awareness goes a long way in healing. Until you become aware of your actions and emotional responses, you are simply acting unconsciously, like being on autopilot. It is hard to change anything when the autopilot is on.

We encourage you to spend the next few days with this assignment: Just be aware of what you are feeling and why. Do your emotions and thus responses to situations come from love or fear? Simply observe and notice this. Do it from an unattached space of non-judgment. This is a way to gently begin getting familiar with your emotional patterns. Don't worry about trying to change anything at first, and do not judge yourself or feel guilty over what you may discover. Guilt is counterproductive to your growth. Just begin this gentle awareness process and see what comes. From there you can begin digging a little deeper and rooting out the core issues. This is when the work can get messy. You may feel like you're in the emotional trenches! This process of discovery can lead to painful memories that you have blocked out or to old emotional wounds—things that hurt you in the past. This process may involve some tears. If that is the case, let them come. Crying is a very effective method of cleansing and can be very healing.

When you do this kind of self-discovery work, the process may be painful, as old baggage is dredged up, but the rewards are worth it tenfold. This is a process of liberation and you will feel much lighter and freer from having gone through it.

We don't want to spend too much time on this subject of emotional self-evaluation and healing. We feel that those who are reading this book already have a basic understanding of this process. We feel you already likely have the tools you need to get started (if you haven't already) and don't need a long discourse on the subject. If you feel you need more in-depth information on how to release your baggage and therefore stop being triggered in certain situations or by certain people, there are plenty of good self-help books on the market right now that can help. Hay House publications, in particular, has quite a nice selection of books that can assist you with this process.

≈ 5 ≈

The Earth Curriculum

THE NATURE OF YOUR SOUL is to learn and explore. You are, by your very soul nature, exploratory creatures! You are each navigating your life with your intended lessons leading and shaping your experiences. Each of you came here with a job to do. You wanted to explore certain characteristics of the earth realm and by so doing expand your consciousness. To that end, you each walk your very own unique path. Yet you are all in this together with one common goal—expansion of the self.

Each and every person, despite appearances, has lessons that they are working on. If you find yourself judging or being critical of another, take notice because that is a lesson for *you* to be working on. When you see another and start to judge his path or condemn her choices, please be aware that their path is just as sacred as yours. *All* paths serve a purpose. *All* of you are contributing to the expansion of the whole. Those individuals who get judged and criticized most are actually fantastic teachers! They provide others with the opportunities to practice love, tolerance, and respect. When you look back over your life at the people who have given you the most trouble, do you see that you learned a great deal from them and grew as a person as a result of your relationships with them? Everyone in your life has a gift for you. Sometimes the gift isn't pretty and shiny, but a gift is still a gift.

When another person acts unkindly, or in a way that irritates you, they are showing you where your triggers are so that you may become aware of areas that need healing. Think of such people as God in disguise. It is common, in fact preferable, for most people to blame others for how they feel. Usually when one feels upset he or she can easily point a finger at another as the cause. Think of it like this, whoever that finger is pointing at is the person to give a silent little "thank you" to. They are showing you yourself.

They may be showing you an aspect of yourself that behaves in the same way they did; they may be showing you an area where you have biases or a skewed perspective. They may be showing you that you have unresolved baggage with someone from your past. Whatever it is, it's *yours*. The wise one will not blame another for "pushing their buttons," but rather will realize that individual has graciously showed up in their life to help them see where their buttons are. This goes both ways. Can you recall instances where you were speaking and/or acting authentically and from love and yet another became angry or upset or defensive? You were helping them see *their* triggers. You are all helping each other all the time in this way. From the guy who cuts you off in traffic to the grievances you have with your spouse, you come into one another's lives to help each other grow. The Universe is always giving you exactly what you need, when you need it.

This process of learning is very effective, but it can seem frustrating when you are unaware of it. Let's say, for example, a person has a problem with change. Suppose they have become very rigid and inflexible because they work very hard to maintain sameness all the time. The Universe will provide this person with opportunities to let go and embrace change. However, if this person continues to be resistant to the opportunities, life may feel very frustrating to them as they continue to resist the opportunities for change. And the more they hold onto their need for sameness, the more opportunities will be presented, perhaps increasing in intensity until the person becomes aware of the need for change.

Remember in the beginning we said you all come into this physical lifetime with a well thought-out game plan regarding what you wanted to learn and how you wanted to contribute? Your soul never forgets this agenda. For instance, if one of the lessons you chose to work on in this lifetime is compassion, you will find yourself continually presented with opportunities to learn about and grow from compassion. You have your curriculum planned and the Universe helps you achieve your goals by giving you continual learning opportunities. Think about when you learned long division. Your teacher gave you repeated opportunities for practice, tests, more instruction, more opportunities for practice, and so on. This is the same process you work through for your life's lessons. Life is your teacher and gives you opportunities to learn in a multitude of ways.

There are four main ways that you are presented with learning opportunities in the earth realm: relationships, work, money, and world/cultural affairs. Relationships are fertile ground for learning. Any time two or more people come together, each with their own respective baggage or agendas, opportunities arise for learning how to love, be patient, be kind, speak your truth, be who you are, be understanding, and be supportive. Whether you are conscious of it or not, you each take on a role when you enter a relationship or social situations. You take on the role of listener, perhaps, or maybe the one who needs to be the center of attention. You step into these roles and then often become resentful toward the other person or people if you are not feeling fulfilled. If you are shy and take on the role of listener, for example, you may feel resentful that you never get to talk. If you take on the center-of-attention role, you may become resentful that you feel you always have to carry the conversation and keep things going.

We encourage you to examine what role you are playing in your interactions with others and *why*. Are you afraid to speak because you fear the judgment of others? Are you afraid you won't get noticed and will consequently feel like a "nothing," so you force yourself into the limelight? What is behind these roles you play? Do you desperately want people to like you so you take on whatever role you think will be most accepted in any given interaction? Are you trying to please everyone? Are you trying to dominate everyone?

There is no need for judgment or shame in any of this. We can't repeat that enough! This is a difficult curriculum, remember? So do not be hard on yourself when you examine where your actions and motivations are coming from. When you look closely and honestly at what roles you play in your interactions with others, see what is at the core of that behavior. What is the reason you are playing that role? Can you feel okay letting that role go and being your authentic self? If not, why not? What is it that you are afraid of? These are all questions to sit with and examine. By doing so, you can learn to let go of the fears or needs that drive your behavior and instead embrace your authentic self.

Another wonderful teacher is money. Money is an energy like anything else and it is neutral, neither good nor bad. Yet it is rare that people view money as neutral. It is either classified as evil or it is exalted. People constantly look at others and see how much money they have and then make all kinds of judgments about the person based on their income. There are judgments about the poor and judgments about the rich. If someone has more money than you, it is tempting to judge him or her negatively out of envy. If someone has less money than you, it is tempting to judge yourself as better than him or her. Money offers all kinds of opportunities for learning and growth!

We understand that your economy is set up to be driven by a "more is better" mindset. You need money to buy the things you need and the things you want. But people have almost become enslaved to money. People give their power over to the "almighty dollar." This term alone signifies how important it is in your culture. You create opinions about yourselves based on what is in your bank account (or what isn't). Self-worth has become tied to money. People who have a lot of it can either feel like they are better than others or they feel guilty and ashamed. So many feelings about the self arise from the relationship with money. You are not your bank account. You are not the car you drive or the house you live in. Likewise, it is unfair to judge or criticize another for what is in their bank account, what kind of car they drive, or what type of house they live in.

It is an important truth to remember that money is neutral—neither good nor bad. Some people may have chosen to experience financial trouble and/or struggle in this lifetime, while others may have chosen to be financially secure in this lifetime so energy could be focused on other pursuits or so they would have the means to support other lessons they need to learn. You don't know what the bigger picture is. It is inappropriate to judge when you do not have all of the information.

A very common misconception about money is that the "haves" are better than the "have nots." This couldn't be farther from the truth. Money was originally introduced into society as a bartering tool; it was intended to take the hassle out of the exchange of goods. The problems the world has now in relationship to money have nothing to do with money itself, but rather with people's ideas, perceptions, and beliefs about it. This has led to conflict and strife, as beliefs such as "more is better" or "haves are better than have nots" have led people to pursue money at the expense of their happiness. Entire nations fight over money. Money itself is not the problem. The problems arise from people's attitudes about money.

Work is another main source of learning opportunity in the earth realm. You are all groomed from a very young age toward careers. Young children are constantly asked, "What do you want to be when you grow up?" The seed is planted very early. Like money, the workforce is another place where a hierarchy of better than/less than has been established. Stand a doctor and a garbage collector side by side and who gets the most votes for being "successful"? Is the trash collector truly less worthy than the doctor? Strip them of their roles and then they are equal, right? But as soon as those job titles are applied, their worth changes in the eyes of society. Even within the same profession, this hierarchy exists. The receptionist of a large corporation is not viewed the same as the CEO of the corporation. To which one do people attach more worthiness? Learning to value yourselves and value others is a large part of what people come to the earth school to learn. It is difficult to do this when society has been set up with these hierarchies and belief systems about job positions and amount of income. Is a waitress acknowledged with the same respect as a priest? A person can be admired and respected for their work, but it does not make them any more deserving of respect than anyone else. You are all divine; you are all glorious souls!

To diminish a person's value simply because of the job they do is an unfortunate distraction from the truth that you are all equal. The trouble is oftentimes that you confuse the person with their job. Let's look at the arena of professional sports as an example. We understand that many people are disgusted by this profession where athletes get paid millions of dollars to play a game, while other people in what you deem more noble professions get paid minimally. Perhaps the *system* itself is out of balance. We won't argue with that. But the tendency is to then judge the athlete negatively because you dislike the field she or he is in. If you pluck that person out of their professional athlete role, what do you have? Simply a human being, like everyone else: a human being no less deserving of love and respect than anyone else. But if you detest the profession of pro sports, you immediately criticize all of those involved in that. It gets into an issue of morals and ethics. The judgment that follows is that anyone involved in a profession you deem amoral or unethical is by association themselves amoral and unethical. This is a snap judgment and may not be true at all.

Regardless, *all* people are deserving of love and respect simply because they are human beings. Again, you don't know what the bigger picture is. You don't know what another is attempting to accomplish on his or her life's journey. You don't know what choices they are faced with and their intimate reasons for making their choices.

We can use the same example of professional sports to examine the other end of the spectrum. There are many who exalt athletes and consider them heroes. They are revered and admired, and people clamor over one another to get a peek at them or to obtain an autograph. They have been deemed celebrities; people are very enamored with this label. So take a famous athlete, for instance, and put him or her in another profession, as a bank teller. Would people still be taking their picture and scrambling for their autograph if they were a bank teller? No. So you can see that the love and admiration has absolutely nothing to do with the actual person at all! It has to do with their professional label. Society has created a system where certain labels can equate to a celebrity status type of admiration or to mockery and criticism. Think critically about this and see how much of your opinion about people stems from what they do for a living. If they had a completely different job, would your opinion of them be the same? If your favorite actor were instead the person who handed you your coffee every day at McDonald's or Starbucks, would you still be so enamored with him or her? Would you even care about them?

Attaching a person's value to their job is a common practice. But it is not a true statement of their value. All people are truly created equal and there is nobody who is more valuable or less valuable than anybody else. Learning to separate the person from the profession and honoring *all* people equally goes a long way in restructuring a system built on false values. When you begin to look upon all others as an expression of the divine, offering unconditional love toward them, a new value system is created, one that is in resonance with your higher self.

Our final point of discussion regarding your most common means for learning is the relationships you have with your world and your culture. The world's population has grown to a very large size; within this enormous amount of people many different sects and cultures have been born. People are very segregated by their differences. Many people still have this sense of "otherness" in regards to cultures very different from their own. This sense of otherness is a barrier that prevents the awareness that you are all the same from permeating your conscious mind. In creating these barriers, your world has become a very segregated place. Such a strong sense of otherness has developed that it is common to feel disassociated from other human beings. This is how people can invade countries and kill others without the bat of an eye. That sense of otherness has become so strong that people have become desensitized to human life, especially if it is a life they do not relate to. These divisions exist all over the world. No specific country is to blame. In every corner of the world, people relate to what they know and disassociate from the rest. Human life is not valued if it is a part of that otherness that is not understood. This otherness mentality drives decisions that world leaders make, it drives decisions that individuals make, and it teaches the children of the world to perpetuate this "us versus them" culture. With such a large variety of cultural expression in your world, a lot of conflict results as the human mind has a strong tendency to want everyone else to do things their way. With so many different ways of doing things (worshiping, eating, living, thinking), people come in conflict out of their judgments of how things "should" be done.

You can see these barriers at play even within your own culture. Just within your culture alone, look at all of the different possible religious expressions. While religious tolerance has vastly improved, you can still sense the rift between different denominations. People tend to identify so strongly with their religion that they cannot believe another way might be just as valid as their own. Whatever faith a person identifies with does not change the fact that each and every one of you is an expression of the divine. This is the bottom line and really the only truth that matters. If this one core truth were to be embraced by all, nothing else would matter. It would not matter what church a person went to or if they went at all. It would not matter what their political affiliations are.

When you see everyone as God and treat everyone as God, everything else falls away. Do you feel you have reached a point of awareness where you know enough to question God's actions? This is essentially what people are doing when they separate themselves from others. The divine is expressing itself in every conceivable way here on your planet. Do you feel you have the authority to question the divine's motives? This is not a reprimand in any way. It is simply a way of looking at things differently and in a more realistic light. You are all tremendously loved and exalted. We are not accusing you of doing anything bad or wrong. But we do wish for you to understand the greater truths at work in your life. Having a more spiritually informed opinion as you navigate your life's journey puts you in a more centered state of grace. By recognizing each and every living thing on the earth as a manifestation of the divine, the barriers and sense of separateness begin to fall away. Through unity your world will become the place of peace and harmony that you desire.

All of the aforementioned vehicles for learning—relationships, money, work, and cultural/world views—offer lessons both at the individual and global levels. These four vehicles for learning are the most prominent teachers you have in the earth plane. There is, however, a much wider variety of "courses" to take than just these four. Let's use the example of a school course schedule again. When you go to high school or college, certain courses are a given—math, English, history—but beyond those courses you may then choose what suits you and what best prepares you for your particular future. A student who wants to be a doctor will load up on biology and anatomy classes. The aspiring writer will have a course load full of English classes. So while there are some common areas of study for all, you also have a highly individualized course of study. Your blueprint for life is not so different.

What you are working on in your life and the areas for growth you have chosen may be very different than your spouse's or your neighbors or your friends. Some people have chosen to be parents; some have chosen not to be parents. Some have chosen to travel extensively to support their particular plan of growth and experience; some may not ever venture past their city limits. That is not to say all things are set in stone. Free will plays a large part in the directions you go in life. What your blueprint for life determines is what specific areas of growth you want to explore—for example, self-worth, judgment, compassion, honesty, humility, poverty, patience, and love. You choose your parents, your nationality, your gender, and your sexual orientation prior to reincarnating. You choose the life circumstances that will best support your overall plan for growth and learning. You partner with the individuals who will support you and offer you opportunities for growth—from your parents to your siblings to classmates to romantic partners to co-workers. Your soul will choose the circumstances that maximize your opportunities for learning your intended lessons.

That said, let's look at your methods for learning. Since you do not have a conscious recollection of your course schedule when you incarnate, you are walking somewhat blindly through your classes. We mean this only in the sense of your conscious mind. There is a deeper part of you that is fully aware of your overall intentions, but it would not behoove you to have conscious memory of this bigger picture because if you did, your learning opportunities would be diminished. And so, you incarnate into this beautiful earth realm with a fabulously designed blueprint for your life that you forget all about once you get here! At least consciously. As we said, at the soul level, you have full awareness of your game plan. So, with no conscious recollection of why you are here, you set about your life. Certain situations will repeatedly present themselves to you. If you pay attention, you will notice these things that keep coming up and say, "Aha! There is one of my life lessons!"

When these things come up for you, how do you handle them? What "mode" do you go into when faced with challenges? Do you get defensive? Do you fully trust and allow the experience to unfold? Do you go into blame mode? Do you go into victim mode? These so-called modes are your current methods for learning. Back to the school scenario: You all had different methods for learning your lessons, yes? Some read every word of their course book and highlighted key points; some skimmed the major topics in the book only; some only read the chapter summaries. Some people needed peace and quiet while studying, while others needed the music up loud. In terms of your life lessons, you have your particular methods for processing and assimilating your experiences. Some people may journal about their experiences, while others may meditate or spend time in reflection about their experiences. You each have your methods. If you go straight to the bar and drink heavily so you won't feel or think about your experiences, this is a method too.

Your methods for handling life may be helpful or harmful to you, depending on what they are. So just as it is important to be aware of what types of lessons are showing up in your life, it is equally important to be aware of how you approach, deal with, and process these experiences when they show up. There are always lessons within the lessons. How you *handle* a particular experience is just as much an opportunity for learning as the experience itself. For example, if your preferred method for dealing with an experience or situation that is difficult or painful is to try not to deal with it at all (via drinking, going on a shopping spree, taking drugs, or vegging out in front of the television), that in and of itself is a lesson. Your methods can give you great insight into yourself.

Many people adopt their parents' methods simply because that is what they were taught through observation. But you are not your parents, and you are now old enough to choose your own methods. Take a conscious look at this and see if you have unconsciously adopted your parents' methods for dealing with things. If so, are they working for you? Is there another way you could approach life that would be more fulfilling for you? If you changed your methods for dealing with life, how would your life change? Could you bring more ease and grace into your life simply by shifting your viewpoint and your ways of approaching and processing your experiences? Experiment with it. If your current methods are not working for you, try something new. Start small if you feel overwhelmed. Pick one particular scenario in which you'd like to change your method for dealing with it and experiment with new methods that resonate more with your heart. When you do this, focusing only on one area at first, and have successful results, positive change will naturally start expanding outward to other areas of your life.

There is no dramatic shift that need take place right now, today. When people see a need for change and growth in their lives, sometimes the tendency is to get overwhelmed in thinking they need to change every single imbalance immediately. Don't worry about this. Just focus on the one area that has caught your attention and work on that. Focusing on a single area that you would like to change allows you to be fully present with that one task and to really become aware of all the little nuances involved. You will likely see that once you put a spotlight on an area and begin working with that, it will be like an onion—multi-layered. When you really pay attention and begin to notice, you will see how this one particular issue is showing up in parts of your life that you weren't even aware of. This is not to be a discouraging practice, but rather very liberating. The most difficult component of change for most people is seeing aspects of themselves that they do not want to acknowledge. People have a hard time admitting to themselves that they have behaved (or are behaving) in ways that are not nice.

We again want to reiterate that you are here for the purpose of learning and growing, so do not feel bad about what you find when you begin to closely examine yourself. You are not expected to be perfect. You would have no need to incarnate if you were. If you begin to feel discouraged or down on yourself, remind yourself that the reason you are even acknowledging your behavior is out of a desire to be more aware, to change and expand your consciousness, which is good not only for you but for the whole world. It is commendable, this spiritual work! And it does not have to be drudgery. Be careful not to wallow in anything for too long. See what you see, feel what you feel, and move on. There is no need to create another set of issues by wallowing and not moving on. This will only create stagnancy.

Another important point to note if you are going to take a good close look at yourself is the need for honesty. Honesty goes hand in hand with what we were talking about before—the difficulty of admitting certain behaviors. When you realize you have been acting a certain way, the tendency may be to immediately begin justifying the behavior. This is a defense mechanism and it prevents you from honestly and wholly seeing your true actions and motivations. It takes strength and courage to be completely honest with yourself and look closely at those parts of yourself you do not really want to admit are there. Again, this is powerful work and it frees you to live more in balance and in harmony with your authentic self, so do not beat yourself up about it! Let go of any notions that you "should" be a certain way and simply acknowledge how you *are*. Then be clear about how you want to change. What changes would bring you more into a full expression of your divine spirit? What are you ready to let go of? What are you ready to embrace? Perhaps make a list if it helps you get clear. The noblest thing you can do in your life is let go of all that does not serve love and expand that which does. That does not mean you are going to live on a cloud and ride unicorns! We are being very practical here. It is absolutely possible to embrace love and yet still feel emotions of anger, sadness, frustration. The range of emotions is part of the human experience. But when you begin to heal and expand, anger can be a fleeting experience instead of deeply rooted. Sadness comes with a greater understanding of life and does not dwell in you forever. When you bring yourself into balance and align with your higher self, the emotions and experiences you have can be navigated with grace and ease.

Learning and growing is a lifelong process. Do not put the pressure on yourself that you need to heal every imbalanced aspect of yourself right away. We do not want you mired down in that kind of pressure and expectation. It is important to enjoy yourself too! While this is important stuff, you do not have to get too heavy with it. Remember to live, to laugh, and to have fun! Love yourself—you are beautiful.

The last piece of our discussion about this before switching gears relates to the nature of your self-image. What is the nature of your self-image? What is your overall relationship with yourself? Is your worth attached to the image you portray to others? When people begin embracing change and self-discovery as we have been talking about, an obstacle that is often encountered is the fear of change resulting from a fear of how others will perceive the new you. If you have created an image or identity for yourself that you feel no longer resonates with you, there may be a feeling of insecurity about changing that identity too much because that is what others have come to expect of you; it is who they are used to relating to, and it is predictable. A lot of people want to embrace change and express a deeper part of their being but they are worried that this will cause discord or negative judgments in their relationships. When one begins to change and blossom and open up to that divine space inside of them, it can sometimes feel threatening or unstable to their loved ones, especially romantic partners. That is okay. What is important to understand is that this is *your* journey, nobody else's, and that your first priority is *you*. It does not suit you to be someone you're not, or tamp down your own growth and expression to keep someone else feeling comfortable.

It is common to feel tied to the self-image that is projected to others. A person's self-image is built largely upon social and cultural factors that do not support the notion that you are all beautiful and divine. In many cultures, humans have a tendency to focus on their perceived flaws and negative feedback instead of their positive attributes and compliments. This focus on the negative versus the positive has become hardwired in the brain so that it has become automatic. Like we said previously, the neurons that fire most frequently in the brain create pathways that become standard operating procedure. It is never too late to create new pathways, though—that is the good news! To do so, one must make a conscious effort to shift his or her attention—in this case to positive feedback and a positive view of the self rather than a focus on the negative or on insecurities.

Often a person develops a carefully constructed image that they portray to the outside world that does not necessarily align with their true image of themselves. Sometimes one who has a negative self-image and feels very insecure will present themselves as incredibly confident and may go to the extreme, where they behave in ways that are arrogant or conceited. In this example, if this person decided to change and wanted to let go of all false pretenses and express his or her authentic self, there may be a sense of fear over letting their guard down, since they have for so long portrayed this image of confidence and self-assurance and this is what others have come to expect from them. There may be a deep feeling of vulnerability in letting that projected image of false confidence go and just being his or herself.

You have been socialized to appear certain ways to gain acceptance and approval from your peers and the society in which you live. So our question to you is this: Is the self that you portray to others in alignment with your true self? Or do you try to portray a self that will be liked and/or admired? It is always a good idea to assess where you are before you decide where you want to go.

The nature of change is that it invokes a lot of other emotions along with it. Fear is often the predominate one. When people decide to change some aspect of who they are, there is then a tendency to worry about how this change will affect their lives and their relationships. Change is a natural and inevitable part of life; resistance to it usually adds undue stress or pressure to the situation. If the automatic reaction to change is worry and fear—either high or low grade—then one can begin building new pathways in the brain to respond to change with faith, trust, and positive expectations. It is simply a matter of consciously shifting your attention and awareness from fear to love. With repetition, responding to change from a place of love and trust will become automatic. These pathways in your brain we speak of are like muscles—the ones you don't use will weaken and the ones that get the most use are the strongest.

Change is a naturally occurring part of life. Having a negative relationship with change only creates stress. To change various aspects of the self—which in terms of spiritual growth really means allowing certain thoughts, feelings, and behaviors that do not align with your divine nature to fall away, thereby making room for aspects of your divine nature to shine through—is a natural part of your evolutionary process as a spiritual being.

≈ 6 ≈

The Law of Attraction and Manifestation

THE EVOLUTIONARY PROCESS of human beings involves going through eras of particular learning phases. It was not so long ago that people were killed for their beliefs, or even accused of having beliefs they did not and killed based upon those false accusations. You have come a long way. When you see the turmoil taking place in your world today—the violence and religious fanaticism of the Middle East, for example—think about how far you have come. The earth is a place for learning and the exploration of a large spectrum of human emotions. Instead of taking a perspective about how bad things are, think instead how much better things are now than they were. You have come a long way since the days of the Salem witch trials, Pol Pot, and Hitler. We encourage you to look at all that is right and beautiful with the world rather than all that is painful in the world.

The world will not know peaceful harmony until its inhabitants decide to embrace this individually. It is impossible to create a peaceful society with constant negative thoughts about that society. The foundation that your world rests on socially, politically, economically, and environmentally will be established by the beliefs, thoughts, and feelings of the majority of its inhabitants. It is not enough that the majority *wishes* the earth were a peaceful place. They must *demonstrate* this desire for peace by aligning with that energy and living in a way that is peaceful. Our example of Sally, who wants peace but becomes irate when she watches the news, is an example of not being in alignment energetically with peace. If you wish to create something, what you are generating with the energy of your own thoughts, actions, and feelings must resonate with that which you wish to create.

The mechanics of energy is simple: Like attracts like. Since all energy carries a particular vibration, in order to manifest any given thing, energies of like vibration must come together. A person emits an energetic frequency with every thought, feeling, and action. All of the above are energy and each thought, each feeling carries a particular vibration. When energetic vibrations are in resonance with one another, they attract. You can do some basic study on quantum physics if you wish to go into this deeper. There is now some very readable material available that explains this law of attraction and the nature of energy.

The path that each and every one of you is on is a highly personalized path designed to fulfill your particular goals for this particular incarnation. When you recognize that some of the same stuff keeps showing up over and over in your life, you can begin to examine this more closely and become aware of how this law of attraction is at work. What experiences do you keep drawing to yourself? Do you see common patterns in your relationships? Jobs? Social life? These patterns are big indicators that these are the lessons you chose to include on your path this time around. What you are putting out there at an energetic level has a lot to do with the experiences that come into your life. We will use relationships as an example because they provide such fertile ground for learning. When a person wants to draw a lover into his or her life, the focus of their energy and the energy they exude will play a large part in who comes into his or her life. A person who is very self-conscious or insecure is likely to attract a mate with the same attributes; like energy attracts like energy. It may look very different in each person, as each may manifest their insecurities in very different ways, but the roots of those expressions are the same. One person may appear very shy and self-conscious and the other may appear incredibly confident. This may look like polar opposites and it may be confusing on the surface to see the law of attraction at work. However, if both of their respective behaviors (shyness and confidence) are rooted in insecurity, that is the common energy that attracted them to one another. Some people may appear incredibly confident to overcome and mask feelings of deep insecurity. That is not to say that all confident people are insecure. This is merely an example of one way that insecurity may be expressed.

When you look past the surface and see what is underneath, it is easier to determine how the law of attraction is working in your relationships. Another aspect to this is the energy you put out there through your mental/emotional focus. When one wishes to draw a mate into his or her life, they tend to focus on the qualities they wish this person to have. It is common for people to make a written list of what they want in a mate. This is a process in manifestation. Manifestation works a little different than the law of attraction.

When you wish to manifest something in your life—a mate, a job, a home—the key factor is concentration. We mean this in the sense that your energy is concentrated on a single focus and not diluted by other thoughts—namely the things you *don't* want in said mate, job, or home. When one develops a manifestation list, he or she has taken all the available criteria and whittled it down to exactly what matches their needs and/or desires in a mate. This concentrated list is then where their focus goes. They concentrate their energy only upon the items on their list and do not give energy to any factors outside of that. By focusing energy on these areas only, a person is exercising their creative control. You are all creative beings and it is the energy of your thoughts, beliefs, feelings, and behaviors that create. These are your creative tools.

The path you are on will determine what types of experiences will predominately show up in your life. A person in need of learning tolerance for example, will be offered numerous learning opportunities in the form of their experiences to master tolerance. That said, the *way* the experiences show up will largely depend on this creative process of manifestation and the law of attraction. Because of the law of attraction, a person will largely be drawing to themselves experiences that resonate with the energy they exude. Prior to your incarnation you designed a blueprint for your life that detailed the particular areas of growth you wanted to focus on. But what is left rather open in the creation of this blueprint is how you will come to gain those lessons. Free will dictates that you have creative control in your life. So when you come into a physical body, with your soul awareness of what your intentions are for this lifetime, you set about your path with the free will to go in any direction you want at any given time, which will certainly alter how your experiences come to you. They depend on which roads you take. The same lesson can be offered through a thousand different scenarios—all dependent upon the choices you make.

Your free will is working hand in hand with a predetermined blueprint for your life. When you wish to obtain a thing—a job, a house, a car, a mate—you spend a great deal of time thinking about the object of desire. The nature of those thoughts will influence the outcome and the timing of the outcome. If the thoughts fluctuate between affirming and hopeless, it will muddy the waters of the creation process. Conflicting thoughts (energy) are being directed at the object of desire. When one is looking for a mate, it is common to fluctuate between thoughts of "I know he/she is out there and I will find him/her soon" and "I'm never going to find the right one." Sound familiar? This is the nature of the mind. It reflects what a person is feeling in any particular moment (hopeful or despondent) through a steady stream of thought. Both the thoughts and feelings are energy and therefore creative tools. So if one desires a particular thing in his or her life, it is imperative to align his or her thoughts and beliefs with the attainment of that goal. This is how the law of attraction and your creative process works—one draws into his or her reality that which he or she transmits.

The process of manifestation is slightly different than the law of attraction. The law of attraction deals with the energy you are exuding at the most base level of your being. It is oftentimes not even something one is conscious of. Many people are not fully aware of what they are putting out there because they are not fully aware of their selves. It is common for a person to view his or herself through rosy colored glasses. This is an ingrained defense mechanism that many individuals have that prevents them from looking at their true behaviors. How many people do you know who behave in ways you would term "selfish" or "greedy" and yet they are not even aware of it? Defense mechanisms are very powerful and often lead a person to justify his or her behavior in order to view their actions in a more positive light. When one is unaware of what they are truly transmitting to the Universe, it is difficult for them to see how the law of attraction works in their life. A person who behaves in ways that are greedy may continually attract to them others who are greedy or other experiences of greed. If this were pointed out to this individual as a potential mirror of their own behavior, and they are unaware of their own true behavior, they will reply that the law of attraction is absurd because they do not at all view themselves as acting greedy. You see, to see the law of attraction at work in your own life, you must be fully and honestly aware of what energy you are exuding.

So how is this different from manifestation? In the larger scope of things they can be considered one and the same. However, when the two are at work here in the earth realm they can be differentiated based upon the origin from which the energy emanates. One tends to manifest from a person's thoughts and emotions (which are in constant flux) and the other from a person's *being*. It is a slight distinction but one that does indeed make a difference.

Let's use our friend Sally again for an example. She is a kindhearted, compassionate, caring, and generous individual. But on this particular day she feels miserable. She is having a bad day and just feels cranky and grumpy. On this day, her thoughts and feelings may be less than loving, as they are coming from a space of irritability. Sally is exuding energy in alignment with frustration and irritability in the form of her thoughts and feelings and may manifest from this space and add more frustration to her day. It would likely be minor things like stubbing a toe, encountering traffic jams, dropping and breaking dishes, or other trivial yet annoying experiences. Sally is not likely, however, to draw a mate to herself who is cranky and irritable by nature because this is not her true nature. Rather, Sally is by nature kind, caring, compassionate, and will be inclined to draw relationships into her life based upon that energy. Do you see the difference? Both are similar in the sense that experiences and/or situations are drawn to a person based upon the energetic vibration they put out. But the origin and nature of these vibrations can be very different and therefore have very different effects. Recognizing the distinctions will help you gain a better understanding of your creative process and how to control it consciously versus unconsciously.

Your manifestation skills are in use all of the time. Whether or not one is conscious of how they are creating is another story. Becoming consciously aware of this process will allow you to create more thoughtfully. It will be easier to avoid unwanted circumstances and draw into your life more favorable circumstances. This does not mean you will never have an unpleasant experience ever again. Some things are meant to occur in your life to assist you on your path of learning and exploration.

When one becomes aware of their manifestation capabilities, it becomes easier to create more thoughtfully. When an individual realizes that thoughts and feelings are creative energy, they begin to become more conscious of their thoughts and make an effort to focus their thoughts in a more loving way. Learning to focus your thoughts in a way that aligns with love rather than fear will result in a far more pleasant human experience. When unpleasant situations occur, one who is aware of their creative power will use the focus of his or her attention to navigate, negotiate, and process the experience with more grace and ease than one who is unaware of their ability to co-create their reality.

We say co-create because you are not working alone. The Universe is constantly conspiring in your favor to assist you in your reasons for being here. Because those reasons have been forgotten, it can be difficult to understand why you are having certain unpleasant experiences. Be assured that without them, you would not have the growth that you came here for. The reasons you chose to experience particular situations may remain unknown to you, but what you can know is how those experiences help you become a more full expression of your divine self. You can see how they have helped you grow, and when you do this, you eliminate the need to experience that particular situation again. It is far easier to navigate your path with the knowledge that you have the ability to use your experiences to your advantage and choose to learn and grow from them.

In challenging times it is helpful to put the manifestation skills to use to determine just how painful the experience really has to be. A person can make any situation more or less challenging by their choices in how to respond to it. One can manifest quick and graceful resolution or one can manifest a long, drawn-out process. Again, it is largely dependent on how a person chooses to focus his or her thoughts and feelings about a given situation. A person has complete control over how he or she chooses to roll with any situation. The situation itself may be out of his or her control but how they deal with it and what they gain from it is completely up to them. Choosing to ignore the lessons present in a given situation will result in future situations presenting themselves that contain the opportunity to learn the given lesson. The Universe is helping you fulfill your reasons and goals for coming into this incarnation. It will do that by presenting you with opportunities to learn the specific lessons you chose to work on. This is why, if you look back over your life, you will notice patterns. Perhaps the opportunity to speak up and use the voice has continually shown up in one's life. This would indicate a need for growth in the area of speaking up for oneself. You are completely aware of all this at the soul level. There is always that part of you, albeit unconscious, that is fully aware of what you came here to do and what paths will serve you best. That part of you guides you to experience the things you need in order to fulfill your game plan.

When one realizes that they are creative co-creators of their life experiences, they may begin to wonder why certain things do not turn out the way they intended when they were using their manifestation skills consciously and to the best of their ability. There are other factors at play, such as divine timing. Remember, you are *co-creators*. You are co-creating with a Universe that is continually working for your greatest good. If you are trying to manifest a mate, you might expect them to show up rather quickly, when in the grand scheme of things it may not be beneficial for you to begin that relationship until a later time. The reasons for this could be numerous. The point is, divine timing will certainly play a role in your life experiences and that is your co-creator's area of expertise. The saying "timing is everything" is quite accurate, and plays a very big part in when things show up in a person's life. Something you can do in regards to timing (since this is really your co-creator's area of expertise) is to add to your manifestation process the intent that what it is you want will show up when the timing is right for all concerned. With that intention set, you can let go of *when* things will happen and simply allow the process to unfold as it needs to. We will cover this topic of divine timing later on.

◈ 7 ◈

Conscious, Subconscious, and Consciousness

THE PHENOMENAL THING ABOUT human discovery is that you do it all with complete forgetfulness of where you came from and your true nature. You tend to look upon yourselves with misgivings and judgment, but the work you are doing is not easy—in fact, there is tremendous difficulty in the "earth school." You are not aware of just how brave and strong and resilient you truly are! You left the freedom of spirit to incarnate into a physical realm that lacks the comforts and ease that you are used to. You do this *willingly* because you are so incredibly committed to your path of spiritual growth.

Every person on the planet has made this brave choice to take on a physical body, forget their true reality, and enter into a realm full of both joyful and painful possibilities. You each made this decision and you each made it from a desire to grow and expand in your awareness. When you leave the realm of spirit to enter into a human body, you leave behind all conscious memory of your true home and why you chose to incarnate. It is like setting out on a great journey and then, just as your boat leaves the port, you realize you forgot the map. Now of course, your soul remembers everything and through intuition guides you along your path. You also have helpers from your home in the spirit realm who look after you and help you to achieve the experiences needed to fulfill your plan. But when you stop to think about this, do you not see how amazing and wondrous you are? Do you see how brave you are? And it is not as if you came to earth blindly. You have had numerous incarnations here, exploring different facets of the human experience. So you *know* how difficult it is here! And yet you still choose to come back, because as challenging as it can be, you are committed to your learning and spiritual growth. Pretty amazing, yes?

So we urge you to remember this when you are feeling down on yourself and judging yourself harshly for some mistake. Trial and error is the way of learning here in the earth realm. You can learn from your mistakes without beating yourself up. You are marvelous cosmic travelers!

That said, let's talk about the nature of consciousness here in the human realm. The terms "conscious," "subconscious," and "consciousness" have been thrown around so much that much of their true meaning has been lost. Your conscious mind is that which you are fully aware of and acting upon with full awareness. It is the part of you associated with your brain and brain activity. It is the part of you that is fully aware of what you are doing and why you are doing it. When you are fully conscious of your emotions, thoughts, and actions, you are operating from this more superficial aspect of the self—superficial meaning not the deeper layers of self, but rather the part of you that you are most familiar with. This is the part of you that you identify with—your so-called personality.

Your conscious self is the one in charge of doing your daily business—getting you safely around town, getting you through your work day, and so on.

Your subconscious is not so readily accessible in terms of your awareness. You are also continually acting and making choices based upon the information in your subconscious, but you are typically not aware of it. You may respond to a certain situation in a way that feels very automatic, almost programmed, and this indicates that you are acting based upon information at the subconscious level. This isn't always information regarding your current lifetime's past hurts and fears, although those are in there too. But the subconscious part of you also carries awareness of your past-life experiences. This can explain why one may act irrationally to a situation that may otherwise elicit little to no reaction. One may be responding automatically to unresolved fears from past experiences in his or her other incarnations. They may or may not be consciously aware that their reaction is out of proportion to the situation itself.

Your soul carries with it complete knowledge of *all* of your experiences. When lessons are learned and awareness is gained, that is incorporated into the soul's current expression of itself. Those areas of unresolved fears and lessons that have not yet been mastered may serve as triggers in the soul's current incarnation. The soul is incredibly expansive and the amount of information it has is inconceivable to the human brain. You have no context for it in the earth realm. The physical vessel that is the human body would have difficulty holding and processing that amount and type of information. It would overwhelm the nervous system to the point of shut-down. That is why the full awareness of your soul is not available to the conscious part of the human mind. Not only would it be overwhelming, it would detract from your lessons in this incarnation. It would be difficult for you to learn if you already had all the answers!

The subconscious aspect of your being carries an imprint of the experiences you have had in other incarnations. It will to some extent color your experiences in this particular lifetime. You can access some of this information through hypnosis and meditation, but the purity of the information uncovered can be altered, as it runs through the filters of the conscious mind. This can especially happen in meditation, as the conscious mind is not being completely bypassed but is still very aware of what is going on. The conscious mind's job is to process, categorize, and sort information based on its current knowledge and understanding and previous experiences in a way that makes sense and can be understood. As it tries to do this with information it has no context for, you can end up with a somewhat distorted interpretation of information you received. In the case of hypnosis, the theory is that the conscious mind is bypassed altogether and the subconscious part of the self is directly accessed. While this may be so, you still encounter the issue of the conscious mind trying to process the experience *after* the fact. A good example of this type of phenomenon is when a person has a direct experience that is spiritually profound, yet completely outside of his or her belief system—for instance, receiving contact from a deceased loved one. As time goes on after this experience, they come to write it off as imagination, or a dream, until it is completely forgotten or dismissed. Despite having an experience and actually witnessing with their own eyes something like that, the conscious mind will try to "make sense" of the information based upon its current knowledge and understanding (which may be heavily influenced by religion, societal beliefs, and cultural beliefs) and will eventually come to the conclusion that the experience must have been a dream, for the conscious mind has no reference for such an experience and no context for placing that experience in its current paradigm.

This can also be the case following a hypnosis session. A person may access all sorts of information through a session; however, when that session is over and they listen to the recording, their conscious mind may run that information through its current filters and leave this person with a skewed interpretation of the experience and/or information received. The more disconnect there is between the information held by the subconscious and the paradigms held by the conscious, the more filters there are for processing the information, which makes the information more distorted. Many spiritual experiences are interpreted incorrectly for this reason. The conscious mind tries to make sense of things that may not adhere to the physical world's laws of physics at all. This can lead to misinterpretation as the brain tries to fit an experience that is outside of your physical world's accepted reality into the paradigm of accepted reality. As your conscious mind expands its awareness, allowing for a more expansive belief system, it will come into closer alignment with the information held by the subconscious. When this happens, accuracy and clarity improves as one interprets spiritual, or metaphysical, experiences they may have.

Consciousness refers to the "aliveness" that is in all things. Consciousness is a manifestation of the divine. It expresses through a various array of forms. Your consciousness does not cease to exist when you leave the body at the moment of death. Consciousness is still a part of you when you are in non-physical form. It is therefore capable of expressing through the form and formless. Consciousness, like everything else, is energy. It manifests itself in a variety of ways to elicit the most expansive experience possible. It is literally the divine expressing, witnessing, and exploring through you and through all other forms and non-forms. When you are in a physical body your consciousness is focused here at the physical level. It is this concentrated focus of consciousness that allows you to be in physical form. When you choose to take on a physical body, you focus a large part of your consciousness on the physical body; you condense your consciousness into the physical form and physical realm. You do not, however, typically focus *all* of your consciousness into this form. It does not require the full concentration of your consciousness to incarnate. Therefore, some aspects of your consciousness remain in the spirit realm or perhaps in other expressions of self in other planes while you are simultaneously here in a physical body on earth.

The entirety of your consciousness is not in this physical body that you are currently identifying with—the one holding this book. There are other parts of your consciousness in other realms. This allows you to have simultaneous, multifaceted, and multidimensional experiences. Now how amazing is that? If you are ever inclined to feel small and insignificant, remember just how expansive and wondrous you really are! As we said, you are quite the cosmic traveler!

Consciousness works through you to gather, grow, express, and expand. It is the part of you that is seeking to know itself. It is the part of you that drives you to gain a deeper understanding of yourself and of life.

Consciousness fulfills the need for expression and expansion on all levels, in all aspects of creation. Consciousness is what animates any given form. Therefore, all living things have consciousness. Inanimate objects are energy, like anything else, and contain trace amounts of consciousness, as all energy comes from a source of consciousness, but not the level of exploration and expression as in animated forms. If it were so, your tables and chairs would be living things and seeking to express and experience. Consciousness, to some extent, permeates everything. However, the degree to which any particular thing contains consciousness is dependent upon the concentration and focus of the consciousness going into that thing. This means that tables, chairs, rugs—they all have a certain degree of consciousness merely because they are energy, and to some extent, all energy contains consciousness. However, consciousness does not typically seek to explore through rugs, chairs, and tables. Therefore, when such an object is created, there is not a heavy concentration of consciousness intent on going into that object. The learning opportunities are minimal to nil and consciousness does not express inefficiently. It will seek to express through animate forms and non-forms because this is where a richer experience lies.

Consciousness can be linked to spiritual awareness. The term conscious relates to the brain, the term subconscious relates to the deeper levels of mind, and consciousness relates to the soul. As a soul grows and expands in awareness, the consciousness of that soul shifts. It becomes more aware. Consciousness is divine energy that is permeated with awareness. It is alive; it is knowing. It is what brings a soul awareness of itself. You look down at your body and see hands, a belly, arms, toes—all your physical attributes that you can identify with as being human. Your brain sees these physical attributes and is responsible for categorizing that information into your awareness of your body.

But what about when you don't have a body or a brain? When your soul leaves the body at death, you are no longer physical, but ethereal. How do you know yourself, know your experiences, know what is going on? Consciousness is responsible for this knowing. Consciousness embodies all the knowledge of who you are and where you've been. It is a knowing that is completely different from the brain's way of knowing. It is an *energetic* knowing. This is why past-life experiences can be carried over into other incarnations. Cell memory occurs when consciousness enters a physical form—thereby permeating the physical structure at the cellular level, infusing the cells of the body with the memory of previous occurrences that can cause the cells to respond to those memories, even though there are no current triggers to elicit such a response. Birthmarks often occur this way. Cells may be infused with the memory of some past trauma at that part of the body and believe they are currently experiencing that trauma and thereby respond to the trauma as if it were current. The cells may die or mutate, just as they would if they were experiencing some sort of abnormal interference. When a past-life memory is carried over to another lifetime in this way, the person may experience fears or phobias that do not make sense to them. A person may, for instance, have a grave fear of imprisonment, although his or her current lifestyle lends no risk to such an outcome. When one recognizes a fear or phobia as a past-life memory, instead of a current threat, he or she may begin work to resolve the fear. Sometimes conscious awareness is enough to flip the switch. Oftentimes, more work will need to be done because even though the person may recognize the phobia as past-life trauma and realize there is no current threat, the memory can be embedded at deeper levels of the being. Simply knowing one is safe may not be enough to eliminate the fear or phobia. Psychosomatic therapy may help a person to release the memory at the cellular and/or emotional levels. Other methods for healing may include regression therapy, hypnosis, visualization techniques, and meditation. Depending on how debilitating the phobia is, one may wish to seek the help of a trained professional in dealing with it. Traditional counseling methods may not be of assistance, as many counselors are not trained in this area of regression therapy and typically lack the belief system or paradigm that supports past-life memory.

As you see, consciousness stays with you—it *is* you, really—as you travel from lifetime to lifetime and from physical world to non-physical world. There are many various forms of consciousness, all serving the same purpose, which is to know and expand and experience itself. For example, consciousness may be expressed in the form of a flower, a bee, a tree, a river, or a person. All living things have consciousness and all are various ways of experiencing the whole. All consciousness is really one—a slice of the divine. But it can express itself and have individuality as well. This is the meaning of "you are all connected." The divine consciousness that all stems from has split itself into various fractals of expression and through those fractals is gaining a deep and rich experience of the various expressions of life. The light that resides in you, that truly *is* you, is this expression of the divine. You *are* the divine. It is expressing itself through you; therefore there is no way to be separate from it. We are using the term "divine" to mean the overall consciousness/creator/energy from which all else exists. It is neither good nor bad in nature because it is neutral—labels cannot be attached to it. This creative energy, which permeates all things, is seeking to express itself in every conceivable way imaginable in order to know life in every facet imaginable. Why? This is expansion, and expansion is the nature of energy. Energy is not stagnant, but a constant ebb and flow, expansion and contraction.

The contraction part comes into play when all the various forms and expressions recede from their current experience and are drawn back into the source. When life ceases to exist at any physical level and that energy is drawn fully back into the divine matrix, this is contraction. From there, a new cycle of expansion will take place. Please do not equate this to cataclysm. It is a natural cycle of energy mechanics we are talking about here. If this information sounds scary to you, it is simply because you have formed a strong attachment to your identity, which you equate to individuality, and this information threatens your existence as you currently understand it. There is nothing to fear, nothing to worry about. We promise you that.

This is some pretty heavy information that is difficult for the human brain to process. It is far easier to understand when you leave the physical plane and return to the non-physical plane, for here you have a greater perspective that is not inhibited by the rational human mind. Trust us when we tell you that you *do* have knowledge and an understanding of all of this and—there is a part of you that understands the nature of your existence and this understanding eradicates fear. It is a current lack of understanding that produces fear. When death releases you from your current body and you go back home to the spirit realm, this will all make more sense to you. As we said, you are limited in understanding due to the processing capabilities of the human brain. There is nothing wrong with this. If it was all meant to be understood, the human brain would have been designed with different capabilities. All is as it should be.

8

Your Multidimensionality

WHEN YOU RETURN TO YOUR HOME in the spirit realm, your perception is far more expansive and clear than when you are in a physical body. You have a greater understanding of the nature of your existence and your purpose. You are not completely cut off from this when you incarnate; in fact, you often travel to your home in the spirit realm during sleep. Your soul can get a lot of work done when your body is sleeping and the conscious mind is off. You do not typically remember your travels when you wake, at the conscious level, but your subconscious does. You are a multidimensional being, meaning you are capable of existing in multiple dimensions. You travel to a different dimension when your body sleeps and your soul "pops out" and goes to the spirit realm, for example.

Remember earlier we said that your full expression of consciousness is not focused on the current physical form that you identify with? Other aspects of your consciousness have focused in other locations. Perhaps some are physical and some are not. You see, you are a multifaceted, multidimensional being. You are exploring and gathering information through multiple expressions of your consciousness, not just this human body you are currently aware of. How cool is that? Truly—you are a cosmic traveler!

Imagine that your soul, or consciousness is represented by a pitcher of water. Now, if you take the pitcher and pour some water into several different vessels, you have a representation of how your consciousness can be focused in several different locations. If you pour each of the smaller cups of water back into the pitcher, you see a representation of what it's like when all aspects of yourself re-integrate.

This representation of your consciousness also mirrors the larger picture—how the divine is expressing different fractals of itself and how eventually all of these aspects of the divine will reintegrate with the whole. By focusing your consciousness in multiple places simultaneously, thereby having multiple simultaneous experiences through different expressions of your self, you mirror what is going on with the divine consciousness, as it has sent out multiple aspects of itself and is expressing through myriad different forms and non-forms. So as there are fractals of the divine expressing itself all over the Universe, there are fractals of your self exploring different realities simultaneously. You are a microcosm of the macrocosm. The same design and intent is present in both.

When you gain insight in one of your realities, it actually shifts your vibration in *all* of your realities. Your consciousness may be "split off" into different realms, experiencing several different realties, but it is still completely connected—it is all *you*. So let's say you gain great insight and awareness through an experience you have here on earth. Let's say that insight shifts your vibration. Since you are not truly disconnected from all other aspects of your self, that shift in vibration will affect all aspects of your self. The vibration of your consciousness as a whole will shift, not just one component of it. As a multi-dimensional being, your experiences in any given reality will affect all other aspects of your self. This may not occur consciously, in fact it rarely does; however, knowledge gained at one level of your being will integrate at all levels of your being. When insight is gained at one level, that insight will carry to all parts of your consciousness, regardless of where these fractals of consciousness are.

These fractals that we refer to can be at different vibrations. Just because they stem from the same source does not mean they have to have experiences of similar vibration. What this means is that it is quite possible for an aspect of your self to be living here on earth in your physical body and carrying a particular vibrational frequency, and another aspect of your self to be experiencing a different reality in a different plane at quite another vibrational frequency.

Since you do not typically focus all of your consciousness into your current physical body, but rather some remains in the sprit realm, or "the other side," which is your true home, that aspect of your self and the current aspect of your physical self obviously carry a very different vibration. The physical you that is here on earth is vibrating at a different frequency than the non-physical you that is still in spirit. By the mere fact that you are in a physical form, your vibration changes from the part of your self that is in non-physical form. Density levels change from the physical to non-physical realms and your energetic vibrations will be in resonance with the realm you are in.

There are more expressions of yourself than just the one here in the physical body and the part of you that is in the spirit realm. You tend to express your self simultaneously in various different realities and all of these experiences of self may carry a different energetic vibration. Again, a lot of it has to do with the density level of the plane you are in. Physical planes are denser than non-physical planes. Different physical planes can vary in levels of density. The denser the plane, the slower the vibration of its inhabitants. Slower rates of vibration are more conducive to particular experiences and faster rates of vibrations are more conducive to their own set of experiences.

This goes back to physics, and the fact that everything is energy and like energy attracts like energy. Emotions and thoughts and experiences are all energy. A plane whose vibration is in alignment with unconditional love would not be a place to experience hatred. The energy of hatred (its vibration) would not match the vibration of such a plane and would therefore not exist there. So, it follows that if different aspects of you are simultaneously in different planes, all with varying density (i.e., vibrational) levels, then *you* would be at different vibrational levels than other aspects of your self.

That said, when one expression of your consciousness gains awareness in a way that raises your vibration, all aspects of your self (regardless of the plane they are in) will experience a vibrational shift. While you can express your self in these multifaceted, multidimensional ways, you are still connected to all aspects of yourself. Your consciousness can focus in different realities, but it cannot truly be separated.

These fractals of your consciousness that have "split off" into various realties (or planes of existence) are never truly separated. Just as the air in a room cannot be separate from itself, you are always connected to all levels of your self and as such continually influence all levels of your self with everything each fractal experiences. As we said before, this design mirrors the larger design of the divine and its infinite fractals of consciousness. It's the same process.

So, if the divine is merely consciousness and energy, how does this fit in with the concept of a loving, benevolent creator? The creation of everything—the Universe, life, all of life everywhere, began from this single point of consciousness. This point of consciousness is full of potential and capable of experiencing anything and everything. You can think of it as a single point of possibility where the potential for all things exist. This means the potential for love and for hate are present. All experience serves a purpose and this point of consciousness expanded its consciousness in a way to experience any and all things imaginable. Love, hate, peace, war, you name it. All is possible. This original point of consciousness was not intent on experiencing only love, in fact not intent on experiencing only one facet of experience at all. That would not provide much of an experience, if only one tiny corner of possibility were explored. And so, as fractals of this divine consciousness were created, those fractals contained the possibility for all things. You are one of these fractals. Ergo, you contain the possibility of all things. Given the entire spectrum of human emotion, it is all available to you. You do not, however, experience all of it. You experience portions of it. You obviously do not experience great unconditional love and at the same time experience hatred so strong you kill someone.

So, although all of the human emotions are available to you and it is possible for you to experience any of them, you focus only on some. There are obviously other fractals of consciousness focusing on other parts of the human emotional spectrum, thereby giving the divine a full experience of all things possible.

That said, let's tie this together to get back to the original question: Is the divine a benevolent, loving creator? It seems odd now that you understand that hate and war are bred from the same consciousness as love and peace. Here is the key. All things are good. All leads to expansion and freedom and the growth of the soul. There are multitudes of ways to accomplish this freedom and expansion, and war and strife are examples of such tools. The terms good and bad and right and wrong are human terms. They do not exist in the true reality of spirit. If only love were experienced and expressed here on earth, people's potential for expansion would be limited. The hatred, the murder, the fear, the war, these are ways that human beings can learn to attain a more loving and expansive perspective. It is the only way. Humans would not learn otherwise. This is what it takes for the human race to become aware, this large spectrum of emotion playing out, from peace to war.

So, in this sense, the divine consciousness is intent on growth and expansion that leads the soul to an ever expansive, loving vibration. You as humans are not focused on this expansion, but rather on the tools used to attain that expansion. Anything that leads the soul into a more loving vibration is good. Therefore, when war and strife occur and the ripple effects of that lead to greater understanding and more expansive awareness, that is *good*. These things bring people together, teach people how to love, how to have faith, and so on. This is the way of the earth school. And so, despite appearances, the divine creator is working toward the greatest good. Always good. You simply misunderstand the nature of the tools used to propel humanity toward this greater good.

∽ 9 ∾

Reincarnation and the Nature of Time

CONSCIOUSNESS IS THE DRIVING force in all things. It is that "beingness" that resides in all things. One need not have a physical form to have consciousness. As stated before, when your consciousness leaves the body at death, it is still very much intact, even without the body.

Life does indeed go on past the moment of physical death. Death is nothing more than a transition between one reality and another. Leaving the body for the spirit plane and vice versa is a process you have done many, many times. To the soul, it is a well-known and easily understood process. The conscious mind, however, can have other notions. Death is a classic example of where the conscious mind takes information and tries to make sense of it and fit it into existing paradigms and belief systems. People who are taught and therefore believe very strongly that reincarnation is not possible will view death and the nature of the soul quite differently than those who have a strong belief in reincarnation. These very beliefs about death (and what happens next) lead a lot of people to behave the way they do. If one believes there is an afterlife where judgment awaits, he or she will act in such a way to avoid a negative review. People who believe that reincarnation, the afterlife, and the eternal nature of the soul are hogwash may perhaps behave recklessly as they feel this is their one and only shot at being alive. What a person believes regarding this subject can heavily influence their life choices.

So where are we going with all this? We would like to lead you into the topic of reincarnation but first wanted to paint a little picture about the various viewpoints people have on the subject and how those viewpoints shape your lives. The reincarnation process is one that allows the soul to experience any possible range of experience and emotion on the human spectrum. Obviously you are not going to cover such ground in one lifetime alone. Rather it is far more efficient to focus on only a select few lessons in a particular lifetime so they may have your full attention. You plan each lifetime very carefully—mapping out exactly which lessons you'd like to focus on and how you can most successfully achieve opportunities to master those lessons. The family you are born into, the geographical location you are born into, the socio-economic status you are born into—all are chosen because they support and provide opportunities for the lessons you chose to focus on. Obviously these variables will change as the lessons change.

Your blueprint for life is very carefully planned and well thought out. The development of this plan occurs on the other side, when you are in spirit, and you have the assistance of your spirit guides as you create it. It is rather like a student working with his or her parents, guidance counselors, and teachers to develop the best plan of action for college and creating a schedule of classes that will best prepare him or her for their intended goals.

So you have created this fabulous blueprint for your next incarnation and then you incarnate into the physical body, retaining this information at the soul level, but completely forgotten at the conscious level. So what happens next? Most often, one gets completely caught up in the life they are living—they may view hardships as unfair and unjust, without realizing they actually chose this life for a reason. They will perhaps go down many different paths until they find the "right fit"—either in terms of careers or relationships. Life may feel like a floundering, confusing journey. As you travel along your life's path you will meet people and encounter situations that help you to fulfill the goals you set for yourself in spirit. You will gain insight and understanding and grow spiritually as a result. You will continually have guidance from your spirit guides, who helped you map out your life plan, although you may not be aware of their presence in your life. All of this you do over and over, taking on various forms—different genders, different personalities, different ethnicities. One physical lifetime is quite a small blip in the overall picture of your experience.

Whenever you leave the physical body at death and return to the spirit plane, you will review your most recent experiences and assess whether you gained and shared what you had hoped to or whether you still need some more time working on certain things. There is no judgment to this process, just a simple assessment of your journey. You do this assessment with full awareness of all other lifetimes you have had. You see what worked and what didn't. You see what variables served your purpose well and what ones need tweaking. All of this information will help you as you plan your next "lifetime." This is a very basic overview of the process of reincarnation and one that sounds very linear in nature. Let's expound on this now to include the nature of time and your other experiences in other planes. You recall previously we said that you are multidimensional and simultaneously experiencing in several different planes. How does this work? How does this fit into the reincarnation pattern we just described?

First, let's explain something about time. Time and space as you experience them and understand the concepts on earth are not the same as on the other side. The idea of linear time is useful in the earth plane and serves a functional purpose. However, time is not truly linear at all. This is merely a tool you are using in the physical plane. In truth, all things are happening at once. If you need a visual, think of time more like a sphere than a straight line. Imagine the sphere to have a center point with lines extending from this point to the outer edges of the circle, like spokes on a wheel. Say one spoke is 1940s Paris, and another is 14th-century Egypt. You can have consciousness focused on both of these spokes simultaneously. Your experience therefore is not linear, but rather simultaneous. While one aspect of yourself may be experiencing life as a milkmaid in 18th-century Europe, another aspect of your self may be experiencing life as a barrister in 19th-century U.S. while yet another aspect of your self may be in the spirit plane, your true home, and continuing studies from there. You see, you are truly and literally multifaceted and multidimensional. When one aspect of your self decides to incarnate, let's say into this present-day body that you know, you do so with the awareness of what all other fractals of your consciousness are doing. The soul is efficient and does not choose its experiences at random. If one aspect of yourself is successfully accomplishing certain goals in one experience, you will not choose to incarnate with the plan of exploring those same facets of those same goals. You will choose areas for learning that most benefit your overall growth. The body you are in now and this life you are living offers unique experiences and opportunities that are not available elsewhere.

When you travel to other dimensional planes, you do so with the understanding that time is relative. You understand that linear time only applies to particular levels of vibration and that the larger picture contains no such thing as linear time at all. So it is completely possible for you to be simultaneously having an experience in 18th-century England and present-day America.

When you venture into the subject of time it becomes difficult, because you are currently living in a plane that only understands linear time. Without day, you would have no reference for night. With only awareness of linear time, it is difficult to know the absence of time. We can try to explain it as best as we can, but our explanation will be rudimentary. Time in essence is nonexistent. It is a valuable tool and point of reference in certain planes, such as yours. When you incarnate into a human body, you enter the time frame that exists on earth. Yet your consciousness is not totally beholden to these parameters of time. You are aware at your soul level that time is merely a tool and therefore your experience is not restricted to this "current" time frame.

Now, how does this account for "past-life" memories that some people have? Reason would dictate that the events remembered would have had to occur in the past in order to be remembered now. But you have to understand the distinction between your brain and your consciousness. Your consciousness has the awareness of all experiences that you are involved in. When some of that awareness slips through to the conscious mind, the brain will process the information within its frame of understanding, which includes linear time. These snippets of awareness will get processed in the brain and therefore be considered something that happened in the "past," which falls in line with your concepts of linear time. Your brain has no choice but to filter information through the past/present/future, because this is the only understanding the conscious mind has in reference to time. There is no other way for the brain to process information.

So, how does this work, exactly? Simultaneous is a term we use to express the true nature of time but even that is not quite right. It is simply as close as we can get, using your vocabulary to express this concept of time. Let's say you have three fractals of your consciousness on the earth plane simultaneously: one in present-day America, one in 18th-century England, and one in 4th-century China. You are living these three different lifetimes simultaneously because time is more like a wheel than a line, remember? And say the you in China lives out his lifetime and dies and that portion of consciousness goes back to the spirit realm, rejoining your consciousness that has remained there on the other side, your true home. Now you have two different lives in the earth plane, one in America and one in England. Say you wish to extend your consciousness back into a new experience on the earth realm, so another fractal of consciousness leaves the spirit plane and incarnates into a body in 17th-century

Paris. You see, you are able to access these various "time periods" because time is not linear. Otherwise you would not be able to access something that happened in the "past." But there really isn't a past! Only a multitude of various experiences involving different planes or even different eras within the same plane.

Now, if there is absolutely nothing left to learn in a particular era—nothing left to be accomplished by incarnating there, for any soul in existence, that era will collapse and no longer exist. It will no longer be an available choice for incarnation.

There are plenty of avenues for the soul to experience—not all are on the earth plane. Your soul can have experiences on other planets and in other nonphysical dimensions. You are not relegated to the earth alone. Your journeys in the Universe are vast. There are a multitude of experiences out there for you to explore.

As we said, there is more of a cyclical pattern than a linear pattern where time is concerned, hence the pattern of the wheel. But by cyclical we do not mean repetitive. When one chooses to go into a physical form and experience a particular part of your earth's offered curriculum, you enter into a dimension where time is perceived to be linear. However, you are coming from a dimension where you know this is not the case. If your soul chooses to work on a lesson that is really only available during a particular time frame, that option will be open to you. There is also the option of observing a particular event without physically being there. For example, let's say your soul chooses to examine a certain lesson associated with persecution. You may observe the Salem witch trials from your vantage point in the spirit realm to gain insight into the nature of persecution without actually being there physically. In the mind of the human self this would be impossible, because such an event as the Salem witch trials has already occurred and is therefore no longer accessible. This simply is not true.

When a soul chooses to explore and learn various themes or lessons, there are multiple ways to accomplish that. Incarnating into a physical form is not the only way to learn. When you are home in the spirit realm you are still learning and expanding your awareness. You may do this by observing events, as we suggested in the previous example; you may do this by studying the myriad resources available on the "other side"—your home in spirit. Even in spirit you have teachers who help you and guide you. The nature of the soul is to expand and to grow. It is always seeking to gain new awareness and new levels of expansion. This does not mean all work and no play! We understand that when reading this and processing this information through the human mind it may sound like drudgery, especially to those who hated school! But we tell you, your soul thrives on this learning, exploring, and expansion. You could say that this is fun for you! When you leave the body and return to spirit, you will choose to continue learning because this is what the soul does and what brings it joy.

～ 10 ～

Free Will versus Predetermination

THE JOURNEYS YOU UNDERTAKE are very rewarding for the soul, even if the conscious mind is in disagreement about this. The conscious mind might say, "My life is too hard. I am unhappy." But the experiences of that life, high points and hardships alike, are responsible for the expansion of the soul and the spiritual growth that it (you) seeks.

Even if you don't understand precisely why you are having the experiences you are having, if you understand that there is a greater purpose to it all that does serve you, you can relax a bit more and not feel so defeated. Perhaps this sounds a bit like you have no choice in the life you lead—as if your soul has some agenda and is dragging you along this bumpy rocky road to fulfill its destiny despite your grievances. This is not exactly true. This is where free will comes into play and free will is very much a tool of the conscious mind. In every moment of every day, you have a choice. You can choose at any point which direction you go in life. This free will works in tandem with the soul's blueprint, or agenda. *Because* free will is a factor, some things on your soul's agenda for this life may not be accomplished. For every move you make in life you have a choice. The issue can be that people base their choices off of fears or off of other people's wishes or expectations and then feel resentful or unhappy. The key to free will is learning to use it lovingly and authentically. Authentically means using free will to base choices off of what you know to be in your greatest good or off of what your heart wants, rather than fear or other people's expectations. Sometimes this can be tricky. If you are an individual with a spouse and/or children some of your choices will affect the entire family, not just you. You may want one thing but your family members may want another, and in this case the "follow your heart" advice becomes very confusing.

Some choices require looking at the bigger picture of what it is you want. In these scenarios, the key is to ask yourself, "In the grand scheme of things, what serves the greatest good for all concerned?" The answer may require you take action in the present that you don't really feel like doing, but it serves a greater goal that you do wish to attain. Let's use a very simple example. Say you have had an incredibly long and exhausting day at work. You finally reach a point in the evening when all of your work and chores are done for the day and you can finally sit and relax for a brief spell before tucking in. You have been living for this moment. Just as you sit down and put your feet up, your teenage daughter informs you that she can't finish her science project that is due first thing tomorrow morning without one more item, which you will need to go to the store to buy. This is where free will comes in. You clearly have two choices: a) you get up and go to the store; or b) you tell her no and stay where you are. What you want to do is stay right where you are. The last thing you feel like doing is making a late-night run to the store. But when you look at the bigger picture, what you truly want (even more than this moment of relaxation) is for your child to pass her science class, which she will not do if she does not turn in her project. Her getting an F and failing the class and lowering her GPA are far greater consequences than a lost night of relaxation.

So how can this relate to your soul's agenda? Let's stick with our current example. Let's say that your soul chose to work on expansion in the area of "self-centeredness." Because this is a chosen area for growth on your current blueprint for life, opportunities will repeatedly appear until you feel (at the soul level) that it has been mastered. When your daughter walks into the room telling you that she needs to go to the store, this is one of those golden opportunities. Two scenarios can play out here. Let's say you tell her no, you aren't getting up and going anywhere. Free will was exercised, but growth in this area of "self-centeredness" was not achieved. Since growth was not achieved through this opportunity, life will continue to present you with opportunities to achieve growth in this area. Your free will choices will determine over the course of your lifetime how much expansion was achieved in this area. When you return to the other side you will assess your life—without judgment—and in looking at this particular area where growth was intended, may decide you did not fully master that lesson and therefore you may choose to focus on it again in another incarnation. Or you may choose to study a different facet of it. You see, *always* you have free will—even when you are in spirit and deciding what lessons to focus on in a particular physical incarnation.

When your free will choices lead to mastery of a particular lesson, you will find that the repeated opportunities to work on that lesson will cease showing up in your life. This is where the free will versus predetermination debate comes in. Yes, you have predetermined the things you wish to work on in your life. Certain situations, experiences, and people are predetermined to show up in your life. But within that predetermined blueprint you have free will. Your choices in any given situation will then determine which direction your life goes. So free will and predetermination is a dance, one that is waltzed throughout the course of your life. It is not one or the other, but rather they work in tandem. Both are at play in your life. Now realize, your soul has an agenda and wishes to fulfill a certain purpose. As your soul is you, not some spiritual entity sitting apart from you, your free will choices a lot of times will be guided by your intuition, or the gentle nudging of your soul. Your soul knows where it wants to go and will be urging the conscious mind to make choices that will lead it in the desired direction. As the conscious mind is forgetful of the soul's blueprint for life and often very disconnected from the spiritual self, it can ignore these urgings of the soul completely. A lot of people are not adept at recognizing intuition. When there is a very strong mental focus, the other aspects of the self—the emotional and the spiritual aspects—can get ignored. Learning to bring *all* aspects of the self into balance will lead to a more authentic experience of the self and will lead to more balanced choices.

11

Personal Responsibility and Healthy Conflict Resolution

THE WAY TO BRING the self into balance is to place equal value on all components of your self. That means equal value and reverence is extended to the mental, emotional, physical, and spiritual aspects of your being. It is common to thwart one or several of these aspects. The emotional self especially gets ignored, as the mental self tries to justify, rationalize, or ignore the emotional self's feelings or choices. The emotional self often is not allowed free expression. The mental self will chastise it and say it is "silly" or "absurd" for feeling what it feels. This creates a tremendous imbalance of the self, which will lead to choices and experiences that don't truly benefit the overall experience of your self. Does that mean when a stranger at the market ticks you off you should indulge the emotional self and go berserk, yelling and screaming at them? That may very well be what the emotional self wants to do. We wouldn't recommend this reaction, but what we *do* suggest is acknowledging your anger. People will try to mentally "talk themselves down" to try to convince themselves they aren't getting mad, they aren't getting triggered. Instead, acknowledge the feelings you are having. You can say to yourself, "Damn! That really pisses me off!" Allow your feelings to surface, instead of trying to push them away. This doesn't mean you have to physically act out those feelings by yelling at or harming another. Realize that the feelings are *yours* and not somebody else's. If you feel like you absolutely need to give physical expressions to your emotions of anger, find a safe way to do so. Examples include running, weight lifting, hitting pillows or a punching bag, dancing, and walking in nature. Physical movement is a wonderful way to move emotional energy and clear it out of the body. You can certainly address another person's behavior if it continually makes you upset by having a conversation with that person where you express your feelings. But this can be done in a kind and safe way, without physically harming or verbally berating them. If your spouse has done something that is making you feel incredibly angry, we suggest "blowing off steam" first by doing something physical—such as running, dancing, yoga, or weight-lifting—and then having a civil conversation with your spouse about your feelings. What does not honor balance of the self is to pack your emotions down and try to pretend you are not angry when you are.

We also don't recommend trying to make someone else responsible for your feelings. People are going to behave the way they behave. You have no control over that. How you respond to another's behavior is under your control and completely your responsibility. You can feel angered by something someone said or did and you can verbally address those feelings with that person. But how will you choose to do that? Through kindness and respect or through yelling and berating? The mental self may say they deserve to be berated and belittled because it is their fault you are upset. This is a common viewpoint of the mental self in the human realm. It is, however, inaccurate. Nobody is ever responsible for your feelings, no matter what they do. Don't interpret that to mean you shouldn't have certain feelings. Whatever feelings the emotional body has is fine and should be acknowledged. What we are asking you to be mindful of is how you choose to respond to those feelings. They are yours. Will you try to make them someone else's? Will you belittle another because you don't like your feelings?

Recall earlier in the book our example of Sally and her response to the news? Sally wants peace in her world, yet is contributing to the lack of peace through her judgment and hatred of those she sees on the news. The same is true for you whenever you treat someone in a way that is disrespectful. If you want a world that is more loving and more peaceful, then you need to model this in your own life. Authentically—not faking it! That means you do not contribute to the lack of love and peace by expressing your own hatred and rage toward another. It is okay to be angry. It is okay to be *really* angry. But there are ways to deal with those emotions that remain in alignment with the greater good of your planet, while still acknowledging and honoring the feelings of the emotional self. You can't expect nations and politicians to behave in kind, truthful, and respectful ways if you are not doing this in your own life. There is quite a difference between authentic conflict resolution and inauthentic conflict resolution (which usually involves blame, deceit, belittling, guilt-tripping, or disrespect).

By disrespecting one another, you contribute to the lack of peace on your planet. Change begins at the individual level. We are by no means saying that you have to grin and bear it when someone treats you badly. By all means use your voice and stand up for yourself. Your voice is a very powerful tool and it will be fueled by your emotions. You can choose to express yourself in a way that acknowledges the feelings you are having without being nasty or cruel. Loving expression does not mean you are a doormat. You are fully capable of being loving yet firm. Healthy conflict resolution will leave the emotional self feeling heard and validated. This method of conflict resolution has not been modeled for you in your society. You have been taught to inflict harm on the one who "hurt you"—either through words, physical force, or a withdrawal of love. It is an eye-for-an-eye mentality, and you know what Gandhi had to say about that: "An eye for an eye makes the whole world blind." Loving conflict resolution doesn't mean you have to pack your feelings down. You can yell at the top of your lungs, "I'm so mad I could scream!" That is allowing the emotional energy in your body and energy field to move. That is completely different than yelling, "I hate you, you are such an incompetent jerk!" That is not healing, but rather contributes to the very energy on your planet that most of you claim you wish to see healed.

We ask you to try to shift your perspective and when someone upsets you, instead of focusing your anger on him or her, turn inward and try to find out why you are upset (triggered) by this experience. What about the experience is upsetting you? Are you feeling invalidated? If so, why is that pushing your buttons? Why not just bless the person who was rude to you and remain strong in your feelings of self-worth and self-validation? You see, this examination of the self will show you where you have work to do. Others are *helping* you to do this and offering you an opportunity for growth when they behave in ways that upset you. If for example, you have a rock solid foundation of self-worth, nobody else can make you feel worthless or less than worthy, no matter what they say or do. If this part of you feels threatened, then it is a sign that you have some healing to do in that area.

But you have not been taught this. You have been taught that when this part of you feels threatened, it is someone else's fault and to blame them and possibly even retaliate against them. You see, if this is the strategy one follows, no healing is actually taking place and someone else will simply come along and push those same buttons. It will happen over and over until the individual realizes they need to heal a part of their self instead of continually blaming others for how they feel. This does not equate to being a doormat. This does not mean you allow others to say or do whatever to you without standing up for yourself. We definitely encourage having healthy boundaries and lovingly defending those boundaries when needed.

Watching your reactions and responses to the things others say and do will illuminate for you the areas in which you have some healing work to do. When you heal an aspect of yourself, you contribute to the healing of the whole world. You are all connected to divine consciousness, remember? So when you grow, you contribute to the growth of the whole. Nothing you do is a singular process. Everything you do has ripple effects and affects the whole.

When you engage in any interaction with another, you can be mindful of the energy you are contributing to the whole. When you run into an acquaintance in the supermarket, are you smiling and nodding as they are talking while in your mind you are having critical or judgmental thoughts about them? This happens all the time and for the most part people are not even aware of it. Becoming fully conscious of your thoughts, both about others and yourself, goes a long way toward healing. The energies exchanged on a daily basis through your interactions are creative vehicles, either contributing to the development of a more peaceful, loving society or to strengthening the negativity and intolerance that already exists. We want you to understand that the creation of your world—either a loving one or a hateful one—is something that every single one of you participates in.

We want to bring your attention to your thoughts and feelings and what they are contributing to. Many people who are very law-abiding, churchgoing, and volunteer-oriented individuals think the woes of the world are due to the criminals, thieves, liars, and so forth. They may not realize that their own behavior contributes to the chaos in society. Every time they judge, condemn, or criticize another, they contribute to the chaos, not to peace. Every time they belittle or disrespect another (either verbally or in their thought process), they contribute to the chaos, not to peace. Even the most subtle forms of judgment are still judgment. Hating a rapist still emits hate into the world. Do you need more hate in the world? Do you wish to contribute to that? Hate is hate, whether it comes from one who commits a hate crime or from the churchgoer who hates the one that committed the crime. The two are really in the same boat in a sense. They are both contributing to hateful energy. The one who *truly* wants to heal the world will only love. This can be a tall order, we know. But you are capable of it.

When people decide to change at the individual level, being very conscious of what they are putting out into the world, then the world can change. Change cannot happen otherwise. It all begins at the individual level. You are each responsible for the energy you contribute to the whole. Now is the time for turning your focus inward to what you are doing and why. Continuing to blame or scapegoat others is not working. Continuing to harbor thoughts and feelings of hate or revenge no longer serves you. The time now is for self-awareness, self-realization, and personal responsibility. This is the momentum that has been building and driving your world toward change. Your earth is moving into a new era where cyclical violence and blaming others are no longer a viable means of exploration and expansion. You are moving into an era where a higher vibration of experience is made manifest so that you may learn in new ways. Continuing to contribute to the old system will cause a sluggishness and blocks your energetic system. This in turn leads to illness or disease if left uncorrected. That is not a scare tactic, it is just truth. We wish for you to be informed so that you may make informed choices. Every choice you make has a consequence and the choice is always yours (free will, remember?). But you must be fully aware to accept that your choices have consequences. Do not make a choice to be harmful to another—physically, verbally, or emotionally—and then get upset that the state of the world is not as you wish it to be. Create in your own life what you wish the world to be. This is the only way it can happen.

⇒ 12 ⇐

The Emotional, Mental, and Spiritual Selves: Healing and Integration

THE VALUE YOU PUT on your emotions (the emotional self) is relatively low; therefore, not only are people used to devaluing their own emotions but in turn devalue the emotions of others as well. When you are not adept at letting your emotional self have expression, it will be frustrating and annoying to you when others are expressing their emotional selves. You see, the mental self does not understand the emotional selves. Therefore, when one is driven by the mental self predominately, an expression of emotion will seem "stupid" or "silly" to this person and they will not value or honor that expression. This often takes place in your relationships. Often, when one person is upset about something that the other person does not understand, they devalue or negate their partner's feelings. This only adds further complications to the relationship. You need to stop trying to understand or relate to the emotional self through the mental self. It will not work. What you can do is form a positive relationship between the two. You do this by ceasing the judgment and criticism you have toward your feelings. How many times have you tried to power through your feelings—steamroll right over them? You may be feeling one way but your mind says, "That's stupid! C'mon, we're doing this!" Imagine your mental and emotional selves as two people. Would they have a good relationship? Does the mental self speak kindly to the emotional self and support the emotional self? Or is the mental self continually telling the emotional self that its feelings are stupid or silly or senseless?

This relationship you have with your self will largely mirror the relationships you have with others. If you devalue your own feelings, you will likely in turn devalue others feelings. You have been raised in a culture that puts more importance on the mental self than the emotional self and this is not healthy. It creates tremendous imbalance in the self and it creates energy blocks in the physical and energetic systems, which can lead to serious illness. A healthy dialogue between the emotional and mental selves looks like this:

Emotional Self: I'm scared.

Mental Self: Okay. That's valid. You're allowed to be scared. I support you.

What that dialogue will most likely look like in your head is you acknowledging that you are afraid of something and then saying to yourself, "Okay I'm feeling scared. How do I support myself through this?" *without* judgment or criticism. What that *typically* looks like in your head is you noticing a feeling of fear and immediately saying to yourself, "No, it'll be fine, I'm doing this and I'm not going to feel scared!" You try to mentally overcome your emotions, which invalidates your emotions. It doesn't mean you have to let fear (or any other feeling) hold you back, but don't tell yourself you are stupid for feeling what you feel, or try to tell yourself you are not feeling what you feel at all. Acknowledging your emotions—with love, not disgust or criticism—goes a long way in restoring balance and repairing the relationship between your mental and emotional self.

These two aspects of you are literally different energetic structures—like two different "selves," which is why we term it that way. You also have a spiritual self and obviously a physical self. For now we are only going to focus on the mental/emotional relationship because this is where so much imbalance comes from.

The nature of the mental self is to analyze, use logic, and understand. It does not give much credence to things it does not understand. Emotions are not something that will always be easily understood. You may have no idea why you are feeling what you feel in a particular moment. Remember how we said your consciousness carries with it memory of every experience it's ever had and how that consciousness embeds your cellular structure? This is not stuff one is usually conscious of. But the subconscious is aware of it. So something may trigger an emotional response in you that makes no sense to you, because what is being triggered is a subconscious or cellular memory that you have no conscious recollection of.

We are not saying to always act on your emotions or give them free reign. There will be times when to do so is beneficial and times when it would not be. Obviously we don't suggest you honor your emotions by giving them free reign when you feel like smacking somebody. To honor the emotions is to acknowledge you have them, allow yourself to feel them, and do this *without judgment or criticism.* Many people were raised to be kind to others and put others first. Then, if they feel anger or even hatred for someone, they feel like that is bad or wrong so they immediately try to tell themselves that they are not feeling these things. They try to negate or deny what they are feeling. This is not honoring to the emotional body. If you feel hatred toward another, how do you ever expect to heal that if you don't even acknowledge that you have that emotion? Honoring the emotional self is allowing it to feel what it feels without judgment. You do not tell a child that she is stupid for feeling afraid of the dark, do you, even though you know there are no real dangers in her dark room? You realize that to berate this child or tell her she is stupid would be cruel. And yet you do this to yourselves all the time!

Negating your feelings or trying to pack them down is what leads to this detrimental imbalance. Having a healthy relationship between all aspects of your being not only keeps you balanced, it keeps you healthy. You decrease the probability of illness when you are in balance. This is not to say you will never get sick again, but it prevents you from experiencing the illnesses that are surely related to remaining in an imbalanced state. There are other causes of illness and disease as well, but many can stem from packing down and denying the emotions.

There are a multitude of other reasons why a person might become ill. Sometimes it is due to blocks in the energetic system, and sometimes it is part of a person's life path to experience illness. If part of a person's blueprint for this lifetime includes experiencing cancer (if this is an important experience for that soul to have), then no matter how balanced that person is, they will still have the experience of that illness. When a soul chooses to expand and grow through the experience of illness, it is not likely that the experience will be avoided. However, if illness is not part of a person's intended life path, it can still show up, or not, depending on the overall health and stability of their *entire* system. Western medicine tends to work only with the physical system. Unfortunately this is a very limited approach. You also have an energetic system and when there is a block or disruption to a part of your energetic system, symptoms begin showing up in the body. When doctors look only at the body, they tend to miss the true cause of the illness, which does not really allow for a true cure. Doctors who are holistic in approach, meaning they acknowledge and work with both your physical and energetic systems, have a far better chance of successfully treating the issue. Let's say you have a splinter in your finger that begins to cause infection. If you only try to do things to alleviate the symptoms of the infection, without removing the splinter, you are not going to have much success in long-term healing. You must remove the splinter to attain true healing. Removing the splinter and treating the infection is akin to the holistic medical approach. Leaving the splinter in and trying only to treat the infection is akin to the practice of traditional Western medicine.

Getting in touch with your own intuition is a good way to get to the source of any disruption or imbalance in your energetic system. Meditating on this with the intent of being shown what needs to be healed is a good practice in your own self-care. Finding holistic practitioners who understand and work with energy and the energetic system is also beneficial. We are not saying shun Western medicine altogether. Healing has many avenues. If you need to go to the hospital—go! If you are having a heart attack, we are not suggesting you go into meditation in that moment and look for answers. Obviously you will know when you need to seek medical care at the traditional level and when you can work with other avenues. Emergency situations often require the work of traditional medicine to get the situation quickly stabilized. Once stabilized, you may choose to begin exploring other, less traditional, avenues.

Now, an important point to note: Your belief system goes a long way in determining what avenue will be successful for you. Your cells are responding to your feelings, your thoughts, and your beliefs. If you undergo some form of treatment all the while saying to yourself, "This is hocus-pocus; this is never going to work," guess what? You're probably going to be right! Belief plays a tremendous role in healing. Experimental studies have been done that correlate the reaction of the body at the cellular level to the beliefs and thoughts a person has. In essence, your body—at the cellular level—will respond the way you tell it to respond. Your feelings and thoughts all stem from what you believe. This is where your spiritual self comes into play. If you believe, for example, that Western medicine is not beneficial to you, then your thoughts and feelings about Western medicine will follow this belief system. So if you truly want something to work, you need to fully believe it can work. You cannot pretend, either.

Energy cannot be manipulated that way. Your true beliefs, thoughts, and feelings carry a vibration that will draw to you experiences that match that vibration. This is why one person can go to an energy practitioner and walk away feeling fabulous and feeling the changes that occurred, while another who goes to the same practitioner can walk away feeling like nothing happened. You tend to find evidence to support only what you believe and leave any contradictory evidence to your belief system just outside the periphery of your conscious mind.

There are, of course, exceptions to this rule. Sometimes a person really needs a paradigm shift for their growth and purpose, and in such a case may approach a holistic practitioner with the belief that it is hogwash and walk away with an amazing experience of success that totally shifts, or begins to shift, their belief system in a way that serves their greatest good. Remember, you have guides who are helping you to achieve the goals you set for yourself in this incarnation. If one needs a shift in their belief system at a certain point in his or her life in order to fulfill his or her goals, then their helpers will find ways to facilitate that, often putting people in front of this person who can offer the experience of a paradigm shift.

A person's belief system tends to lay the foundations for the thoughts and feelings that person has. Although these things certainly can be out of sync, the thought patterns and feelings one has will tend to follow their belief system. Issues begin to occur as beliefs shift, as they will naturally do through the course of a person's life. Sometimes when a particular belief is challenged and begins to change the mind, the emotions are reluctant to follow and cause conflict. If, for example, a person was raised to believe in the possibility of going to hell, and then, as this person begins to gather information and expand her awareness into a different belief system, the emotional self may cling to the fear of hell even though this person has changed her beliefs about that. Sometimes, as in this scenario, not all aspects of your self are on the same page. This individual may declare they no longer believe in hell and yet still behave in certain ways out of a fear that still resides in the emotional self of going to hell.

So, when different aspects of your self are on different pages, you end up with this internal conflict. It is common for a person to have multiple conflicts going on at once. People tend to be very fractured between their emotional, mental, and spiritual selves. First, just knowing, recognizing, and acknowledging that you have these different components to your being starts you off on the right foot. Next, you need to validate and honor all of those aspects as we discussed previously. Next, you need to integrate these components by bringing them on the same page. When you are in complete alignment between your mental, emotional, and spiritual beings, you have balance. Balance is the foundation for good health. Trying to operate from a belief system that conflicts with your thought system or feelings will lead to imbalance, which sets one up for health issues and conflict.

So, how do you bring these aspects of self into balance? You first must find and address any conflicts that exist within you. What causes you turmoil? What causes you guilt? What feelings or thoughts do you have that are not in sync with what you believe? Or, what thought patterns do you have that conflict with how you feel? Finding the internal conflicts that exist in you is the first step. It is easier to do this when you write it down. Make a three-column list with each column heading containing one component of you (mental, emotional, spiritual). Write in each column what you believe, think, and feel about a particular thing. This exercise alone can give you tremendous clarity. This alone may give you the "a-ha!" you need to make adjustments and bring yourself into alignment. Next, look at your answers and ask yourself why you are not on the same page. For example, if you have written under the "belief" heading, "I believe God loves me unconditionally," and next to that under the "mental" heading you wrote, "I think God loves me unconditionally," and next to that in the "emotional" column you wrote, "I feel maybe God loves me when I'm good but is disappointed in me when I'm bad," you have an obvious disconnect at the emotional level.

So you need to ask yourself why. Why are you emotionally feeling something different than what you think and believe? Is your emotional self still running off of some program you were raised with even though you have long since changed your mind about it? Try to find the origins of the disconnect. Sometimes they will be obvious, sometimes they won't. You can also go into meditation with the intent of finding clarity. Here is an important point to note. As you do this exercise there will be a tendency for the mental self to take over and dominate the process, as is the case with most all pen and paper exercises. Be mindful of bringing all aspects of your self to the table and giving all equal voice. If you try to do this exercise solely with the mind, you will likely perpetuate the mental/emotional imbalance.

The next step is integration. Once you have isolated the cause of conflict you can ask yourself what you need to do to bring these aspects of yourself into harmony. Does a belief need to shift? Does a thought pattern need tweaking? Do you need healing at the emotional level? What will bring all of you onto the same page? This process may take some time as you practice putting the changes into action. It may require breaking out of old habit patterns or long held beliefs systems. That can be an ongoing process that you work on day to day. But as you do so, you can have a supportive and loving relationship between your mental, emotional, and spiritual aspects of being. We would like to offer a meditation to heal this relationship between these aspects of your selves.

Meditation for Healing

Get comfortable and close your eyes. Focus for a few minutes on your breath, allowing it to fill you and gently release from you. Begin to picture a place where you feel happy, safe, and free. Perhaps the beach, a mountain stream, a meadow full of wildflowers. Maybe it is your own backyard. Wherever you are, this is *your* special place—where you find healing, serenity, and peace. Now, imagine seeing four beautiful, radiant, light beings sitting in a circle talking. As you look closer you realize these beings are you. You see your physical body, your emotional self, your spiritual self, and your mental self all sitting in this circle. They have come together to heal their differences and unite with one another. Take brief note of how these beings appear to you. What does the emotional self look like? The mental self? The spiritual self? Allow a dialogue to open between these beautiful beings where each gets to express their opinion. You may hear the physical self state that it does not like being told it is "fat" or "ugly." The mental self may express frustration for some of the things the emotional body feels. This is all done in a very safe and loving way. There is no name calling, no judgment, no belittling, just a gentle sharing of each one's viewpoint. Next, allow each aspect of you to express to the others the gifts it, and only it, shares. The emotional body can tell the group that because of it you are able to feel love and feel joy. It may express that the love you feel for your pet or spouse or child would not be possible without it. It is a valuable member of this team and it is not trying to convince anybody of this but rather allowing the others to see the gifts that it shares. When one is done speaking, allow the next to share and so on. Your physical body may wish to remind the others of the miraculous gifts it brings to your life experience. It allows you to smell your favorite smells, to feel such glorious things as warm sun on the skin or cool grass between the toes. It allows the divine breath to pulse through all of you. It allows you to touch and feel and hold your loved ones. As each aspect shares its gifts, imagine the others hearing the one speaking with full unconditional love, honor, respect, and acceptance. Imagine the bonds of love and friendship growing strong between these four. When each being has finished speaking, see them all hold hands or embrace in a group hug. They now know the value of each other and vow to support and love one another. When one is having an issue the others don't understand, they will rally around and stand in support of this one and get through it together. Allow yourself now the freedom to express any way you choose. Maybe these four want to have a celebratory dance party, maybe they wish to have a scared ceremony, perhaps they wish to walk together and explore this beautiful place of serenity and healing. Spend some time doing what feels good. Take as long as you need and when you are ready bring your awareness back to your breath. Slowly open your eyes and smile! Pat yourself on the back for a job well done!

Bringing the different aspects of yourself into a positive, supportive, and loving relationship with one another is incredibly powerful and will completely change your relationship with yourself and with life. Happy changes are bound to follow! When you bring all aspects of your self into a unified, supportive whole you begin to build a strong and solid foundation of well being that serves to support you in a more healthy and balanced way through challenging times. When you are going through an emotional process, it makes all the difference in the world to have the love and support of your mental and spiritual selves. Loving yourself—on all levels—is the safest, healthiest, and most balanced way to heal. When you love someone, you don't need to understand where he or she is coming from to love and support them. You support them regardless of understanding *because* you love them. This is the type of relationship we are encouraging you to have with your self. When the mind doesn't understand or agree with something the emotional self is feeling, it can still respond lovingly and be supportive, rather than engaging in negative self-talk and criticism. All aspects of your self are valid. They all speak different languages. So you may not always be able to understand why you feel what you feel. Or perhaps you hold a belief that tells you that you shouldn't feel what you feel. Anytime you negate or criticize or chastise your feelings, you are withholding love and support from a very special and important part of your being. Be with this for a while and begin to allow the supportive, loving relationship to unfold.

Crucial to your development is this bonded relationship with your whole being. Without it you remain fragmented and divided. It is nearly impossible to have a joyful experience of life without this cohesiveness. A loving bonded relationship between the components of your beautiful self looks like a loving, healthy relationship between you and another person. If you pay attention, you will see the similarities in how you treat others and how you treat your self. How you view others and judge others is typically a mirror for how you judge and view yourself. If one tends to get irritated by and critical of another person who is being emotionally expressive, for example, this person may also notice that he or she is being critical and irritated at his or her own emotional side. How you view and judge these aspects of yourself will also be how you view and judge them in other people.

Therefore, learning to create a loving and supportive relationship between your different aspects of self not only creates a more healthy and stable foundation for you, but it also allows you to improve your interpersonal relationships with others. When you become patient, loving, and kind toward all aspects of yourself, you will then also be patient, loving, and kind when you see those aspects being expressed by another person. This knowledge of the mental, spiritual, and emotional aspects of self and an awareness of the validity and importance of each is a tremendous key to having a fully authentic and loving partnership with another human being.

When you think about your relationships, you will see that much of the strife arises because one person expresses feelings or beliefs or ideas that the other person does not understand or agree with, and the resulting reaction of this disagreement is often judgment, criticism, and/or invalidation of the other's point of view. This is the same reaction your own mental self often has toward the emotional self. Learning that all aspects are valid, worthy, and deserve expression—whether it makes sense to you or not—is the foundation of a relationship that can bloom into a solid, supportive, and loving union. So many of your arguments stem from invalidating another's feelings. Many people do not feel emotionally heard or validated in their partnerships. This again is because you have not been taught to value this emotional part of the self as much as the mental part of the self. If one is used to invalidating his or her own emotional self, you can bet this one will also do the same toward his or her partner.

People have a need to understand something and sometimes even need to agree with it before they will validate or honor it. The fact is you are not always going to understand your partner's feelings. And you will not always agree with your partner's feelings. That is not truly the point. Before you address the issue of disagreement, it is important and imperative to a truly healthy relationship that you validate and honor the others' emotional self (the feelings that they are having) regardless if they make sense to you. In doing so you are honoring and being supportive of a very real and important aspect of that person's being. You don't have to feel the same way they do and you don't need to understand *why* they feel the way they do. All you need to know is that the feelings of another human being are just as sacred and valid as your own feelings. One of the greatest gifts you can give another person is *genuinely* hearing them and honoring their feelings. This is so rare because the teachings of your culture do not emphasize this at all. Rather, you are mostly taught to judge what you do not understand. You see this judgment and criticism all over the place. People laugh at and make fun of other people for behaving, thinking, feeling, or looking different. That is truly dishonoring. Beginning to see the oneness in all and being supportive and honoring others goes a long way toward a peaceful, cohesive world culture. Loving each other and loving your self does not look very different—it is the same thing. By deepening your relationship with your self and loving all aspects of your self, you become capable of a deeper more loving relationship with those around you. There is no difference between yourself and others and what you extend to one you extend to all. Before we begin a new topic let us make just one more point here. The endless joy and freedom that comes from a balanced, loving relationship with the self is your gift to yourself. Nobody else can give you this. Only you can create an internal climate of love, support, and harmony. When it feels as if you have this because of another's love for you, it is not a solid foundation. If your feelings about yourself, or any particular aspect of your self are based on another's love for you, you are always at the mercy of that person's feelings. The moment their feelings change and they no longer love you, what are you left with? If you have a solid foundation of *self*-love, that will always be with you, independent of what others say or do.

We want to emphasize this important point, because many people base their feelings about their self on how others feel about them. When one is feeling loved and cherished, their esteem is boosted and they feel pretty good about their self. But when that love ceases, they feel awful about their self. Your worthiness is not dependent on how worthy others see you. When one has a loving relationship with the self, it will not matter when another gives and then takes their love away. There may indeed be sadness and other feelings but the foundation of the self remains strong. When you have a strong foundation of self-love, then how you feel or what you think and believe about yourself will not be dependent upon any other person's love, acceptance, or approval. That's freedom!

⁓ 13 ⁎

The Shift into a New Vibrational Range of Experience

THE TIME HAS COME NOW, in this era of awakening on your planet, for expansion of awareness, both awareness of the self and awareness of the bigger picture of reality. The paradigms that have served people for millennia are no longer applicable and are rapidly breaking down. From these shattered paradigms arise new ways of thinking and new belief systems. The children being born today are very different than the humans being born fifty years ago. People are now incarnating onto your planet with greater awareness of their divine self and with an innate desire to serve the greater good rather than just the self alone.

The next phase of your journey as a human civilization includes exploration at a deeper spiritual level and a more profound experience of the self. People are beginning to see the illusions they have lived by and drop those for more authentic beliefs and values. More and more people are beginning to recognize the interconnectedness of all things and their own connection to the divine Source. This is an era of awakening on your planet and as such, new opportunities are being presented to the human population. You are a race that is shifting into a heart-centered state of being and therefore what you experience will be vastly different than ever before.

When one operates from the heart center, life feels different. Everything is approached from a different perspective than before. People are becoming more certain of their choices, their beliefs, their values. When humanity makes a shift as big as this one, everything changes. Entire systems—political, economical, social—will have to be restructured. What was built from a head-centered space cannot continue to thrive in a heart-centered society. The needs have changed too much. When new systems are established, they will be created upon a foundation far different than those that came before. Foundations are now being established based upon the greater good of the community and the world at large. Where money dominated the choices and decisions before, a more compassionate approach is surfacing. Self-serving business plans are being replaced with community-driven business plans. As people become more aware of the nature of energy and their own creative roles in their lives, there will be a decline of the desperate, fear-based decisions and business layouts regarding money. The old paradigm involved making sure one would have money—the more the better—first and foremost and at the expense of others. While financial security will indeed remain an important factor in one's life, obtaining it at the detriment or expense of others is a paradigm that is drastically shifting. People's perspectives are changing with this change to a heart-centered way of life in such a way that the focus of the individual is expanding out from the individual alone to embrace the community and the world. People are beginning to see the importance of serving the greatest good of the whole instead of just the few.

This is a massive and dramatic shift for many of your established systems and we can't say it won't be messy in some cases. That is nothing to worry about. The power of change comes in keeping your focus on the greater good. There may be some small victories by those who oppose this new paradigm as some continue to cling to the fear-based paradigms, but there is no need to despair over it. The momentum toward a shift in all your systems—a shift toward the greater good—is too strong and too far along. Those who fight it will have a tough time. What these individuals need is your compassion. They are the ones who are finding healing most difficult. You can pray for them, or send them light if that suits your belief system. What we discourage is sending them any negativity. The political arena is a tremendous opportunity to practice this. How common is it for one to send love and light to a political figure they are in opposition to? The political preferences of people are fairly black and white—they love one politician and despise another. What if people shifted their perspective so that instead of despising those political figures they do not support, they back them spiritually? How different could things be if everyone supported everyone, whether they agree with them or not? You may only support one politician with your vote and your monetary donations, but you can simultaneously support all the others spiritually and emotionally by allowing the energy of love and compassion to flow freely to them.

There are many different ways to be supportive of another human being. You do not have to agree with someone to support them. The two are not mutually exclusive. One does not require the other. You can be in total opposition to a political figure in terms of your stance on the issues, and yet be supportive of their experience as a fellow human being. What you have been taught is to withdraw *everything*—all respect, kindness, love, and compassion—when you disagree strongly with another's actions and beliefs. You are all expressions of Source and that means that every single living thing on the planet is equal and equally deserving of love and respect. This one basic truth has gotten far lost throughout the years of opposition. People have taken such a strong stance against one another that they have forgotten they are all the same. Awareness of your connectedness and equal value is dawning now as you move from a mind-centered species to a heart-centered species. This nature of humans has long been to view one another as completely separate beings. This is now changing, both at the individual level as people become aware of their divine connection to all things, and in your scientific world as studies are proving this to be true, not just theoretical. You can expect science to take some new and exciting turns in the upcoming decades.

This dawning era of enlightenment, as it has been called, is not one where you will be floating on clouds and frolicking with unicorns. The changes taking place are profound indeed but not what a lot of the human race is expecting. The changes occurring are vibratory in nature, meaning that the vibrational frequency of the earth and the earth's inhabitants is shifting into a new range. The range that was previously available has expanded to include even higher vibrational experiences than before. To understand this, you must first understand that when you are incarnate in a human body, only a particular vibrational range is available to you. We talked of this when we covered the varying density levels of different planes. If for example, your earth plane houses inhabitants whose vibration is in a range of 150-300 MHz, this expansion of range we now speak of means that the range has been "bumped up" from 300-350 MHz. This offers all kinds of new experiences that were not before accessible in the human realm on earth. (Note: these numbers are purely hypothetical for the sake of discussion and should not be taken literally.)

The experiences that reside in that 300-350 MHz range which weren't previously accessible will now become part of the offered curriculum here on earth. The human body has been energetically changing to support this new range of experience. And as we said before, the children being born are already energetically compatible with the new range of vibration on earth. The beginning stages of this shift in vibration were what you may call "messy." A lot of upheaval took place to get rid of the old in order to make room for the new. This was evident on a global level (earthquakes, tsunamis, floods, fires, and tornados) and on an individual level as well. Many people chose to exit the earth plane (via death) and many others have experienced feelings (both physical and emotional) like never before as old baggage came to the surface for release. You see, in order to move into this new range of vibration, the lower end of the range slides up too. So not only has the range expanded from 300-350, but it has shifted up from 150-200 at the other end. What does this mean? It means any and all energy one carries in the form of thoughts, emotions, beliefs that fall within that 150-200 range must go! That energy cannot exist at the higher range.

So let's look at the whole range shift now. Let's say the vibrational range on earth has long been 150-300 MHz. The current shift has caused this vibrational range to now be 200-350 MHz. This means all those things that resonate in the 300-350 range were not available before but they are now, and all those things that existed at the 150-200 range must go because they do not resonate at the new 200-350 range. Making sense? It can be confusing, we know. But you can understand it better when you let go of the need to understand it!

When a shifting in vibrational range like this occurs, people experience the upheaval of anything that energetically resonates in the lower end of the range so they can be in resonance with the new range. This can create illness, either long or short term, random aches and pains, emotional outbursts that are out of character for that person, feelings of emotional instability, and bizarre and erratic behavior. Big changes occurring on your planet inevitably lead to big changes at the individual level. Some will deal with this more gracefully than others. Some understand the process and others don't. Regardless of where one falls on that spectrum, these changes are affecting *everyone*, whether they know it or not. We do wish to clear one thing up. There will not be cataclysm and destruction, as some people believe. There is not going to be an apocalypse situation. The world is not going to end. The 2012 marker indicated by the Mayan culture was not to signify the end; it was signifying a beginning. It is the beginning of a new cycle in earth's evolutionary process.

As this new cycle begins, people will be working with new energies that were not before familiar to them. They may find that what once upset them no longer does, that their expression and experience of unconditional love has reached a deeper level that was not before felt. Awareness is shifting so that esoteric, spiritual truths that may have not made sense before suddenly make sense and are easily understood. As we said, you are changing your energetic structure to be in harmony with this new vibrational range. Your operating system is being upgraded! This affects you at the level of DNA and your cellular structure. Everything about you is changing! Do not be alarmed by this. You will not wake up one day in a body you do not recognize. The shifts and changes taking place are a natural part of your evolution and they are unfolding in a manner that people can deal with them. You are not turning into robots or super-humans that will fly to work instead of driving. Some drastic things about the nature of your reality are changing and science will be disclosing some discoveries and truths that will change the way people operate and view reality, but don't expect to become the Jetsons. Drastic overnight overhaul that would completely freak people out is not going to happen. You are not intended to be freaked out to the point that you can't function.

Let's talk briefly about the comment we made before about some people choosing to exit the earth plane through death. This may conjure all sorts of connotations that are not true, so let us explain this. At the soul level, you are fully aware of when you want to leave the body and you will choose the time and manner of your death with complete awareness. No accidents, no mistakes. As the earth plane is undergoing this dramatic shift in vibrational frequency, some will choose to continue their journey elsewhere. This plane may no longer appeal to some and the lessons they are seeking to learn.

For example, say a large corporation has just been bought out and the new management is going to make extreme changes to the company—a complete overhaul. Every employee in that company has a choice. They may like the new direction the company is heading or they may decide it's not for them and choose to leave the company. There is not right or wrong, good or bad to it; it is simply a matter of choice and preference. One may decide that his or her personal goals and intentions for what they want in their career will be better served somewhere else and leave the company because it is no longer a place that serves their particular career goals. This is what is happening as the earth plane shifts in vibration. Some will align with the new range as it serves their purpose and their goals; some may choose to go somewhere else that is a better fit for their purpose and goals. There is no right or wrong, good or bad to it at all. You all have choice. It may not be evident to you at the conscious level, but your soul is *always* choosing the path that is in your greatest good.

    Some individuals may choose to exit their current physical structure and be born again into a new body in this new earth plane. Given the new opportunities for experience with the shift in vibrational range, it may behoove some individuals to begin as a new body in different circumstances. The soul is aware of this bigger picture—of all the changes taking place and what opportunities that offers and where it is best served. It may say, "Oh look! Now I can have the experience of xyz that would really benefit my growth!" But in order to get that experience of xyz, the soul would need to leave and be incarnated into a different body, in order to perhaps access a different culture or different gender. Perhaps that experience of xyz wasn't available when they incarnated into this current time frame because the vibrational range was different then than it is now. This shift in range opens up a whole new set of experience.

The bottom line is this: Your soul is a highly intelligent being and it knows what it is doing. Therefore, do not view another's death as a mistake, or bad timing, or as an avoidable accident. It is never any of these things. The soul does not leave the body unless it chooses to. So *any* death is a highly planned exit strategy by the soul. This is true whether the person was six months old, five years old, twenty-nine years old, or eighty years old.

The human experience of death provides a multitude of learning opportunities for the bereaved. A soul that has left the body, even in violent, atrocious ways, does so knowing that the experience of their departure will offer valuable lessons to those around them—lessons that *those* souls have chosen to learn. It is a gift. Every death is a gift. No matter the age or circumstances of a death, it is all planned by the soul who is exiting to give the most benefit to those around them. Again, where people aren't conscious of their soul's agenda, this may be difficult to come to terms with. Death is a beautiful thing but has become vastly misunderstood. It is a wonderful vehicle for growth and awareness but as these lessons often come through the emotions of grief and anger and extreme sadness, people have lost sight of the miracle of death. The emotional attachments people form with one another prevent them from seeing death as the beautiful gift and transition it is. What is helpful to understand is that nobody truly dies. People come and go from this earth plane but they do not cease to exist. This new range of vibration on the earth plane will offer new and more expansive experiences around the nature of death that will help people to see this truth. Some of your scientific breakthroughs regarding space and time will also help people to better understand the eternal nature of the soul and your ability to connect with those who have left the earth plane. Death is the transition from one plane to another. As your earth plane is changing dramatically, some will decide they are better suited in another plane and choose to exit this one.

The shifting vibrational range on the planet is causing a lot of upheaval in terms of natural disasters and personal relationships. Let's spend a little time with this in an effort to present you with a broader understanding of what is going on. Anytime a shifting of energetic vibration occurs of this magnitude, large-scale change of the physical structures of the planet result. There is really no other way. Imagine a pot boiling on the stove. There is a lid on the pot and eventually when the contents get hot enough a tremendous amount of pressure builds up. Since there is a lid containing this pressure, it will continue to build until it has to go somewhere. It would build to the point of blowing the lid off the pot and the contents would erupt out onto the stove. This isn't exactly what is happening on the planet (the vibrational changes have nothing to do with heat or pressure) but the metaphor is to indicate that when enough change occurs within a structure, something's gotta give!

The earth is shifting into a higher vibrational frequency and as such it must release any energies not in resonance with this new range. It is the same process you are going through at the individual level. The earth (and its inhabitants) are "shaking up and clearing out." What we really wish to draw your attention to is your response to these events when they happen. It is typical to view such events as catastrophic, devastating, and senseless. The reality is: It is none of these things. Recall our explanation of the death process. No death is accidental. So one factor that people struggle with in the face of these natural events is the idea that innocent people are senselessly killed before their time. It bears repeating, so we will say again: There is no such thing as "before their time." Nobody leaves the body unless they have chosen to.

Another point to note is this: Leaving the body is not a bad thing. This life you are living as a human on planet earth is not your true home. You leave your home on the other side to come to earth to learn, grow, and share. By leaving the body at death, one is simply going back home to their natural state in spirit. So when one understands these truths around "death," it helps one to gain some greater perspective when natural "disasters" occur.

Next, we wish to draw your attention to the nature of these "disasters." That label alone indicates the current human viewpoint on earth changes. The term "disaster" has negative connotations. In truth, a better descriptor for these events would be "natural events" or "earth changes." That is simply what is happening. The earth is in some fashion shifting or releasing or clearing. Despite appearances, this is a positive thing. Change and forward movement are to be celebrated and embraced with joy. Now that is a strong statement when we are talking about, say, an earthquake where many lose their homes and/or loved ones. We are not suggesting you replace compassion with celebration in these occurrences. We strongly encourage responding to such events with love, compassion, and a helping hand. We are not saying you should adopt an attitude of apathy toward these people affected by such events. The pain and suffering that those involved in these events go through is very real and warrants compassion and understanding.

However, it is entirely possible to have this compassionate attitude while simultaneously having an understanding that in the grand scheme of things, these earth changes are not "bad" or "disastrous." They are serving a greater purpose, and it is a purpose that serves the greatest good. People understandably have a difficult time reconciling the idea that an occurrence that serves the greatest good could also cause a lot of suffering for many people. The human brain is not adept at reconciling two very different notions such as this. It has been programmed to make the following equations: suffering = bad, and lack of suffering = good. These are very black and white statements and do not allow a lot of room for any type of grey area. As human beings have a very limited *conscious* understanding of the bigger picture, it can be difficult to think outside the box of those two equations. Let us draw your attention back to our previous explanation of the benefits of the Holocaust. We remind you that that was in actuality a large movement toward tolerance and acceptance. It is hard to see that bigger picture when so much suffering was involved. But pain and suffering and violence have long been some of the primary educational tools on your planet. You knew that when you decided to incarnate here. You left your home on the other side, which is devoid of violence and pain, to enter into a world where such things exist because you knew that they provided wonderful learning opportunities. Once you incarnate, however, you lose this bigger-picture perspective and it all just looks like senseless travesties.

When these natural events, like hurricanes, tsunamis, tornados, or earthquakes occur, you can simultaneously give compassionate support to those affected while understanding that in the grand scheme of things change is occurring that somehow serves the greater good or some kind of forward movement that benefits the whole. Knowing that such events are a movement toward a greater good does not justify apathy or nonchalance toward these events. They are not intended to be ignored but rather are intended to propel people into compassionate action and awareness. Such events as these provide opportunities like no other to help people learn to bond together, support one another, have compassion for one another and so on. Do you see where these are all *positive* things? Without events of such an extreme magnitude, certain experiences of human growth could not be attained. It takes large-scale events to wake people up and propel people toward change. When things happen on a small-scale level, not many people take notice. The small-scale stuff is going on all the time but affects only the few. When national or worldwide events take place, they provide rare opportunities for growth and large-scale movement toward a greater good.

Serving the greater good is the benevolent nature of the divine Source and the energy that moves through the Universe. This is accomplished in different ways on different planes. The earth plane vibrates within a particular vibrational frequency, as we have explained. Only certain experiences are available within that range. If, for example, you went to a plane where the range of vibrational frequency was much higher, violence and suffering would not be tools for learning there. Violence, for instance, would not be in resonance at that level of vibration and would therefore not exist. Your home in spirit is a plane such as this. It vibrates at a frequency that is not in resonance with violence, hatred, or anger.

This is why most people do not typically see their loved ones who have died even if their loved one is standing in the room with them. Your physical eyesight works within a particular vibrational range and does not tend to perceive anything outside of that range. Those who do "see" the dead are very rarely seeing with their physical eyes. They are typically using senses you as yet have little understanding of and therefore no terminology for. The best way to translate the experience is to say they "see" things, although their perceptions are coming through the third eye, not the physical eyeball. This brings us to our next topic, the subject of psychic abilities and extrasensory perception.

≈ 14 ≈

Psychic Abilities and Your Inner Navigation System

PSYCHIC PHENOMENA ARE A SUBJECT of great interest on your plane, so we can spend a little time with the subject. People tend to be very fascinated by those with "abilities" to see and hear and feel things that most people don't. Why is this? Why are only some people capable of such sensitivities and not others? The bottom line is: You are *all* capable. The senses used to perceive these non-physical entities are available to everyone. Some are going to be more in tune with these senses because they are energetically predisposed to being sensitive. The reason for this is typically because they chose prior to incarnating to be of service through the use of such abilities and therefore are energetically set up for such. These individuals will have more of what you call a natural ability to see/hear/feel things in other planes. They may be born with this ability fully activated or it may not be activated until later in their life. Those who have this energetic predisposition are likely to be using it in some way to be of service. That said, even those who are not energetically wired to be "translators" or "seers" still possess the capability to tune into other planes.

What keeps people from experiencing these extra-sensory senses is the amount of "baggage" they carry with them. The emotional baggage people carry clouds these senses and prevents them from "tuning in." One needs to be fairly clear to perceive vibrations that are not native to your plane. In order to be clear, one must not be bogged down with belief systems and emotional baggage that cloud their ability to tune in to other vibrations. Please don't be disturbed by our use of the term baggage. We do not mean it in any kind of negative way. We simply recognize it as a term you typically use and so for the ease of discussion we use it too. The more baggage one has, the less likely it is for them to be in tune with their non-physical senses. Picture a flashlight sitting in the middle of the floor, turned on. It is bright and clear. Now, take a shirt and throw it over the flashlight (baggage piece #1). You can still see the light through the shirt but it has become dimmed, not as clear. Now throw another shirt on the light (baggage piece #2). The light may even still be faintly visible but is obviously becoming more difficult to see. Keep piling clothes on the flashlight and eventually you do not even know it is there. In this metaphor, the flashlight is your ability to perceive things beyond your physical plane. It is your extra-sensory perception. The clothes represent the baggage that prevents you from being aware of that ability. Everyone has what we're calling "baggage." It is part of the human experience. You grow up, you go through various experiences, and the painful ones that caused suffering or fear to arise typically get stored in your being and tend to then be triggered as you go through life. Oftentimes these emotional triggers are so deep seated, people forget or are not aware of where they come from.

Before we go deeper into this, let us explain one thing. There is a hierarchy system in place in your culture where any number of things falls on a spectrum of better than/worse than. We are not fond of this hierarchy system as it diminishes the value of the self, but we see the purpose it is serving in your society. Without it you would not be able to realize your equality. Without being shown lessons and examples of this system of inequality (where some are perceived as better/worse than others), you would not have the foundation necessary to fully embrace true equality. The earth plane is a "school" that uses this method of duality, as it can be a very effective method for learning.

In terms of psychic phenomena, those who are readily able to perceive it are often placed at a higher level than others on this hierarchy scale. They are viewed as special (which humans translate as "better than") and more interesting. We want you to understand that no one person is better than another. Every single living being on your planet is divine. There is nobody who is "more divine" than any other. You all have the same elements of Source within you—you are all *equal* expressions of Source. What happens when one with these psychic abilities is placed on a pedestal or perceived to be better than others, is the people who come to listen to their message get lost in their message and lose touch with their own inherent intuition. In the presence of such people, others tend to give their own power away. It is common for one to completely disregard their own feelings and intuitive urgings and take at face value everything they are told by the one who is "psychic." Yes, these individuals with highly activated psychic abilities are providing a service and do have a valuable gift to offer. But we wish to remind you that *you* are a powerful spiritual being too.

If you are seeking advice from one with abilities, or reading a book written by one with abilities, we ask you to do so with the frame of mind that there is no "better than" involved. Take every piece of advice or anything you read and run it through your own intuitive system. Bottom line is this: *You* are the creator of your reality. All decisions and choices ultimately come from you. You can do what someone else suggests you do—which may or may not be in your best interest—but don't blindly follow another's advice because they are using their abilities and have been placed by you in a position of superiority. Blindly following *anybody* because you have placed him or her in a position of superiority is not recommended. It does not matter how gifted one is or how many credentials one has—if what they are telling you just absolutely feels wrong to you, then honor your intuition and follow your own guidance. This hierarchy system in which psychics have been placed in a superior position causes people to give their power away by not listening to their selves. We are not saying to shun those who can help you or have something to teach you, but we encourage you to stop belittling yourself in the presence of such teachers.

We encourage you to embrace your own navigation system. You may not be seeing those in other planes or acting as a medium, but you most certainly are able to attune to your own inner guidance system. In every decision you make, you can take all the information gathered (whether it came from a psychic or others) and weigh it against how *you* feel. You always know at your core what is the right direction to take, you only need to tune into that and trust yourself. Another may provide you with information that is completely accurate and yet it may not be the right timing for you to act on it; only you can truly determine what is in your greatest good. You are all perfectly equipped with this inner navigation system. It is simply a matter of quieting your mind and feeling what is in your heart center. This heart center of yours is like a beacon of light illuminating the brightest path before you. It is your doubts and fears that obscure this light.

Let's use an example to illustrate our point. Imagine you are walking home from work, tired and hungry, wanting nothing more than just to get home and collapse. As you're walking home, you get a phone call from your best friend, who is devastated because his or her relationship has just ended. Your friend asks you to please come over and keep him or her company. What do you do? People are faced with situations like this all the time and nine times out of ten they go to the aid of their loved ones, setting aside their own plans. In these scenarios the heart generally leads you to the aid of one in need of comfort and support. You make this decision to go to your friend without even thinking about it. This automatic response to go to the aid of a friend is a heart-centered move, one in which the conscious mind plays very little part. After you agree to go to your friend's house and hang up the phone, your mind may begin to get involved as you are making your way to their house. At that point your mind may be thinking things like, "Oh man, I really don't want to be doing this," or "I just want to go home!" But in that split second where you made the decision to go to your friend, none of this chatter was taking place. Your heart led the way.

You have all likely been in situations similar to this and therefore know what this *feels* like. You know how it feels when your heart guides you. In these scenarios, even though you may be exhausted by the time you get home and you may have been thinking that going to your friend's house was the last thing you wanted to do, overriding these thoughts and feelings is typically a deep feeling of goodness and satisfaction. It feels good to be of service and to provide support for those who need it. Despite the consequences, you tend to feel really good about being able to help or being able to be there for someone. This is such a basic example but it is a situation that you are all surely familiar with to some degree and therefore we chose to use it because we know that you can relate to the feelings involved in such a scenario. We are trying to draw your attention to the difference between following your heart and following your mind. Those split-second decisions where you just *know* what to do without any thought involved, that is listening to the heart. The heart knows—it doesn't need to mull things over or analyze. In any situation, it knows which direction it best serves you to go.

The rational mind usually steps in, however, and begins some dialogue that then muddies the waters. Then you don't know what to do—you feel one thing and think another. This confusion causes you to doubt yourself and then you go seeking for answers outside yourself. You pay lots of money for books or seminars or psychic readings, hoping that someone will tell you what to do—that they will give you the answers. These avenues have value and are wonderful tools to use for growth, gaining a deeper understanding, and getting clarity. But the bottom line is you have a well-equipped navigation system within you that has all the answers and is always ready to point you in the direction of your greatest good. You may require assistance at times, but we do not encourage you to denounce your own powerful system of intuition. The answers you are seeking are always within you. You only need to learn how to listen to that part of you that knows. The mind is used to hijacking your other information systems. Be kind to your mind; this is all it knows and what it was trained to do. But you can retrain your self so that your mind begins to quiet down and you become adept at feeling what is in your best interest in any given situation.

When one becomes more clear in his or her energetic field, he/she is a clearer channel for the other side. When one has a lot of baggage or preconceptions or belief patterns that contradict the notion that there is life on non-physical planes as well as your physical plane, the channels get muddy and the conscious mind takes over any incoming information and processes it through its filters. This often leads to people dismissing or negating metaphysical experiences when they happen. Some people, on the other hand, are perfectly open and willing to believe there is life in other planes and yet they still do not receive communication. Why is this? First off, we must remind you about our previous discussion about the conscious and subconscious minds. Much of the communication you receive occurs at the subconscious level—when you are asleep, for example—and doesn't make its way to the conscious mind. You are *all* in contact and communicating with your helpers and guides in the spirit plane. It's just that most of this communication stays at the subconscious level. When the conscious mind gets hold of such information, it has a tendency to distort it as it tries to analyze, process, and make sense of it. The information is being processed through all of the conscious mind's filters, which are based upon belief systems, fears, possibly incorrect notions and ideas, and personal experiences. You can see why your guides and friends in spirit choose to bypass the conscious mind altogether and work with you at the subconscious level.

We don't recommend you spend your time trying to be "psychic" or to communicate with those on the other side. If this is meant to happen, it will. What we suggest you focus on is learning how to tune into your intuition. *That* is useful and beneficial to you. Trying to talk to and see "the dead" or "the future" is typically a desire rooted in ego and that doesn't serve you. What truly serves you best is honing in on your inner guidance system. You run the same risk here of any information you feel with your intuitive sense being warped through the processing of the conscious mind. This takes practice and discernment but you will get a handle on it. You will eventually become familiar with your intuitive feeling center and know when something you "get" is from your intuition or from your mind. With practice and attention you will easily begin to recognize when the mind jumps in and tries to process and distort the information you receive.

Please be aware that people's intuition comes to them in different ways. Some people have "gut feelings"; others will simply "know," meaning the answer to something just pops into their head. Some will see a vision of something in their mind's eye. Here is an exercise we recommend when you are seeking clarity on something or needing an answer to something. Sit with your hands over heart center, close your eyes, and breathe. Take a moment to breathe and relax and calm the mind. Then bring your awareness to your heart center with your question in mind. It is there. You will be able to just "know" or just "feel" what is right. It is important to release attachment to the outcome when you do this exercise, because attachment to certain answers or particular directions in life will cloud your intuition. Just be still, let go, and allow the answer to be there, whatever it is. You have the answers to all of your questions within you.

We want to make a quick point here. We do not recommend you ask questions about others, such as "Is so-and-so cheating on me?" A more appropriate question to ask is, "Is it in my greatest good to be in this relationship?" Intuition is a tool for you to take direction *your* life. Try to keep your questions, therefore, about you. This is not a tool intended to learn about others or delve into the personal experience of others. If you feel another is somehow not serving your greatest good, do not ask about them, rather ask if it is in *your* best interest to be interacting with them. This tool is for you to find clarity on *your* path.

This exercise will get you used to the difference between your mental chatter and your intuition. Eventually you will learn this discernment to a point where you can simply bring your awareness to a question and know the answer. You can do it standing in line at the grocery store or while working out at the gym. Your soul is always guiding you through your intuition. Your soul speaks through your heart center, not your mind. Your intuition, or the communication of your soul, is like that flashlight buried underneath all those clothes. When you take the clothes out of the equation, what you are left with is pure intuition. Pure knowing. Home is where the heart is. If you want to get in touch with your soul—your authentic true self—which you could call your "home," bring awareness to your heart center. The heart whispers while the mind shouts, so take time and have patience as you retrain yourself to listen to the gentle nudging of your soul. If you are trying and trying and not getting clarity on something, just let it go. Let it go and trust you will know when you need to know. That brings us to our next subject—divine timing.

⁕ 15 ⁕

Divine Timing

DIVINE TIMING ACCOUNTS for a lot of your frustrations! We say this sympathetically because we know it can be frustrating to be working within a framework that you don't even know exists. So let us explain this to you now. Divine timing is essential to your growth. Without it, things would be chaotic and you would miss a lot of opportunities for true learning and understanding. If certain information or experiences were to come to you when you were not ready for them, those learning opportunities would be wasted and you wouldn't gain the wealth of knowledge that you *do* stand to gain when such opportunities or experiences are presented to you when you *are* ready for them. It is a highly efficient tool, this divine timing, and it ensures you all don't go through life "half-baked."

Think of it this way: If things just came at you willy-nilly, and you weren't ready to gain anything from them, those experiences would have to keep coming back around until you were in a place to benefit from them. This is highly inefficient, and the Universe is an incredibly efficient entity. Think of your academic setting as an example. You go from K-12 grades, and through the entire course of those years you cover simple number recognition, basic addition and subtraction, fractions, division, geometry, algebra, and calculus. But your teachers don't randomly throw calculus at kids in grades K-5; it would be wasted on them because they are still gaining the foundational understandings necessary to approach calculus. It would be a highly inefficient system to throw *all* forms of math at kids of *all* ages and just see what sticks. Rather, you understand that proficiency must be mastered at one level before proceeding to the next level. So it is with divine timing.

You may think you want something so very badly and you put all of your manifestation skills to use and still it doesn't come to pass. This is the point where people begin to think the whole notion of manifestation and the law of attraction is hogwash. What they are not considering is this very important factor of divine timing. The law of attraction does work. *When* something shows up in your reality is often outside of your control. Remember, you are *co*-creators. We assure you, this is purely for your benefit and never to hold you back or put a damper on your desires. Divine timing works in your greatest good, always.

If you have children, this will be fairly easy to understand. How many times has your child so desperately wanted to do something that was not appropriate for his or her age? You tell your child they must wait until they are older. You aren't doing this to be cruel or controlling; you do it in the best interest of your child, because you have a broader understanding of the situation than they do. The child may not like your decision, however, and may sulk or tantrum for a bit over not getting what they want. Sound familiar? With all due respect, we see a lot of this sulking and tantruming in you grown-ups when something you have been trying to manifest in your life does not come to pass. Let's use another example, this one for adults.

Say Sally is desperately miserable at her job and ready to leave. But she can't put in her notice until she finds a new job. She feels she is doing everything "right" in terms of manifesting—she is aligning her thoughts, her emotions, her actions, all of her energy, with finding the perfect job. Yet nothing happens. Months go by and Sally begins to think that this manifestation business is a load of hooey. She may start to question her powerful creative nature and begin to succumb to notions that she is destined to be miserable. Then one day Bob is hired where Sally works. Bob and Sally know each other *very* well at the soul level. They have traveled many lifetimes together and have agreed to meet up in this lifetime to experience pure, ecstatic unconditional love. Bob and Sally obviously don't know this at the conscious level. At the conscious level all they know is that they have just met the partner of their dreams. They fall in love and live happily ever after. This never could have happened if Sally left her job before Bob showed up. Divine timing, you see. Now that Sally has met Bob, which was an important part of both Sally and Bob's life path, Sally begins to get other job opportunities. Shortly after meeting Bob, Sally finds her dream job and she is free and clear to leave her current job. Divine timing.

Do not be discouraged if things don't unfold for you in the exact manner you wish. You are working within this universal law of divine timing, which is set in place to serve the greatest good. We understand that there are times when you consciously believe that there is not possibly better timing for something than the present. One who has run out of money and is facing eviction and has just had their electricity turned off would surely think there is no better timing for some cash than now. Divine timing works for the greatest good of all. If your life plan involves going through a specific experience, then no matter what you do, it is likely that you will not escape that experience. The one with the money troubles who is close to eviction and without power may have set up this situation in his life plan to experience the lessons associated with this particular scenario. Perhaps these circumstances will force this one to move in with his brother for a spell, which leads to tremendous emotional healing and growth for both parties. Perhaps this was all the point in the grand scheme of things. But as you are not aware of the grand scheme of things at the conscious level, it would seem ludicrous that one would be better served going through such an experience rather than receiving the much needed money. That money may very well come, *after* the purpose of the experience has been served. Divine timing.

You don't have to understand the bigger picture to accept the notion that there is a time for everything and only when one is best served by an experience will that experience show up. Divine timing ensures that you as an individual, and the collective whole, experience only what is in your best interest. It sounds like an infringement on free will, but it is not. That is simply the way the conscious mind wants to interpret it, because the conscious mind tends to rail against not getting what it wants. Divine timing is not an infringement on your free will because it doesn't negate or alter your free will. You might not get something when you want it, but that really has nothing to do with your free will choices. You are always free to make whatever choices you want in any given moment.

For example, divine timing might play a part in you and your "true love" meeting—assuring it happens when the time is most beneficial for all involved—but you can still choose to ignore that person and not get involved with them. If it was part of both parties' life plan to meet and have a relationship, you may see the Universe keeps creating scenarios in which you two keep running into each other. You will continually be put in front of each other (your guides know your soul's intent to have a relationship with this person and they are going to try to help you fulfill that). But what happens with you and this other person will be completely dependent upon your free-will choices, which may or may not sync up with your soul's plan.

You have surely seen examples of this divine timing in your life. If you look back at certain points in your life where you really wanted something and didn't get it—either at all or not until much later—and now from the vantage point of hindsight you see how much of a good thing that was. Either you weren't really ready for whatever it was you wanted, even though you thought you were, or if you would have received your desire it would have led your life in a direction you see now would not have been the best choice for you. Divine timing isn't hard to recognize. It's pretty easy to spot when it's at work in your life. It is only the conscious desire to get what you want that gets in the way of seeing divine timing when it is at work in your life. And of course, like anything, it is far easier to recognize in hindsight.

≈ 16 ≈

The Role of Faith in the Creative Process

RELATED TO THIS NOTION of divine timing is the matter of faith. Faith that everything is happening exactly when it needs to happen is a tremendous tool that allows the fears, doubts, and worries of the conscious self to give way to a more receptive and relaxed state of mind. Faith helps people who are in this situation of not consciously remembering what their overall game plan is, which is the case with you, the human race. Faith is the tool that bridges the gap between the skeptical, unknowing conscious mind and the fully aware consciousness of your spirit. Faith is that tool that allows people to "let go," which is incredibly beneficial. Faith has absolutely nothing to do with religion or any set of religious beliefs. It is a beautiful, spiritual tool available to every human being on the planet, whether they are a devout Christian or an atheist.

You would be amazed if you saw the benevolent helpers all around you who help guide and assist you through your life. You are not all randomly running around playing a human game of bumper cars, bouncing around from one random experience to another. Even the most avid atheist has these benevolent helpers. It does not matter what you think or what you believe—you all have guides in spirit who helped you design your life plan and who help you to see it through throughout the course of your life. They are not running your life for you, but they are helping you to get the experiences you set out to get when you incarnated. Faith that there is a game plan, a grander design to your life than you are aware of, tremendously helps to relieve stress and fear from the mind. Faith paves the way for acceptance. Acceptance of "what is" creates an energetic space that is more harmonious and healthy to be in than fear and mistrust.

You have the notion that anything unpleasant is "bad" and should be avoided. But you have to remember the earth school doesn't operate that way. Growth and expansion of your awareness is achieved through all types of experience—both what you term pleasant and unpleasant. This doesn't mean you shouldn't strive for pleasant experiences in life—by all means yes, you should! But when you hear of some travesty where people were harmed or killed, it is inaccurate to think, "Why did their guides let that happen to them?" You are always in the driver's seat. Nobody else "lets" things happen to you. Through all manner of experiences people grow and learn and gain valuable knowledge and insights. It is not truly accurate to say "bad" or "painful" things shouldn't be allowed to happen. If they didn't serve a purpose that was *good*, they wouldn't be allowed to happen. It's that "big picture" thing again. All of these things you term atrocities somehow, in some way, serve a greater good. Otherwise they wouldn't happen. Faith plays a large role in accepting this truth because when you are having a human experience with complete forgetfulness of the bigger picture, it can be very difficult not to get caught up in the pain and suffering you see and begin to believe it is senseless and pointless. Like we said before, the Universe is very efficient. Things do not happen willy-nilly for no reason.

This idea of faith is not meant to replace your decision-making process. It is not a suggestion to walk blindly into any situation and have faith it will be fine. You are intended to use the tools given to you in your intuition, logic, and discernment. Faith is a tool to be used when you enter into those unknown realms, philosophically speaking, that you have lost conscious memory of. Faith is what allows you to accept and trust that everything in your life is unfolding at the time it is meant to. Faith is not ignorance. It is trusting. It is trust that you are more than your physical body; it is trust that there is more to your life than you are currently aware; it is trust that you are not alone on your journey. Faith is a necessary tool in this human realm where conscious remembering of who you are and why you are here is blocked.

So why this memory loss? Why not just remember where you came from and what it is you intended to do in this incarnation? It seems like having full memory of why you are here would be more efficient, right? That is actually a counterintuitive idea. Believe it or not, it is more efficient to forget who you are and why you are here!

The point of human incarnations, as you now know, is growth and expansion of the self. The best way to do this is to completely jump in or immerse oneself in certain situations. It is the difference between watching a tennis match and playing a tennis match. You come into physical form for an experience that will provide your soul with the growth and expansion it desires. Why do this without memory of your game plan? If you had full conscious memory of everything you would not gain as rich of an experience as you do when this is blocked from your memory. Let us ask you this—if a school student walks in to class to take a math test with the answer sheet in his hand, will he actually learn anything from the test? He likely won't even do the math; he'll just write down the answers. He might get a perfect score, but will he learn anything? If he relies on the answer sheets for every test, do you think he has a full, comprehensive understanding of the material? Your soul *truly* wants to learn and grow and doesn't look for any shortcuts—that would defeat the purpose. You know that if you incarnate with full awareness of your home in spirit and what you came here to do, your choices and feelings would be very different. They would be influenced by your knowledge, which doesn't give you the opportunity of first-hand experience of particular situations and emotions. If you retained full awareness, you may as well not even incarnate! You may as well stay home (in spirit). When you are at home in the spiritual realm, you do learn and explore with full awareness of who you are and all the experiences you've ever had. While the learning opportunities are vast and fulfilling, there are certain experiences that can only be gained in a physical plane. In order to learn in the physical plane you must bring your vibration in resonance with that plane so you have access to the thoughts and emotions there.

For instance, if you really want to learn about envy, at a deep level, you are not going to be able to do that in the spirit realm because that vibration does not exist there. From spirit form you can observe people in physical form engaging in envy-fueled behavior and you will learn a thing or two from your observations, but the only way to understand it and grow from it fully is to actually have the experience of it. For that, you need to go where it is. Again, it is the difference between watching people play tennis and playing tennis yourself. You will learn some good pointers by watching, but you won't fully know what it's like until you play it yourself.

You see, if you really wanted to learn through the vehicle of envy and decided to incarnate and have experiences related to envy, if you retained full awareness you wouldn't even care about envy. You would be at a higher spiritual level of understanding and not engage in envy-fueled behavior because you would not feel in resonance with that. So then what would be the point? By forgetting, you readily engage in the expressions of envy, or anger, or jealousy, or conditional love that you would not be inclined to if you retained full awareness. Your soul does exactly what it needs to do to maximize its experiences of expansion. This "forgetfulness" that may seem frustrating or pointless to you is actually a highly efficient means of enhancing your growth. If you walk into the earth school and you already have all the answers, what do you stand to gain?

This brings us back to faith. With faith you don't need to know why you are here or what your life plan looks like. Faith allows one to be hopeful and trust that those things that on their surface don't seem to make any sense actually do serve a purpose, and the purpose serves the expansion of the self. Before we move on from this notion of faith, let's examine one more aspect of it, that is, the aspect of letting go. Faith is what allows a person to do this. If people tried to understand and make sense of every single occurrence in their lives and in the world, they would drive themselves crazy. At some point faith steps in and allows one to surrender to what is, or simply to surrender to not knowing. Surrender is *not* defeat. Surrender is the tool of the wise. Surrender is a letting-go and allowing process. This is usually where the magic happens!

Think of a time when you were banging your head against the wall over something, perhaps resisting some scenario in your life, or perhaps trying desperately to understand something that made no sense to you. At some point you reached a space of throwing your hands in the air and saying, "I give up!" What you really mean is you are letting go. You didn't stop caring about whatever this scenario was or stop wanting what you wanted. You just let it go. You surrendered. And then, did clarity or awareness come very easily after that? It usually does! It's that old adage, "What you resist persists." Letting go and having faith that there is more going on than you understand and that life is unfolding perfectly allows one to move into the flow of life rather than trying to paddle upstream against it. Letting go without faith can be done, but it is usually faith that allows one to let go.

This sounds very simple and obvious, but when you are actually in an emotionally vulnerable or charged situation it can be difficult to let go. A lot of this has to do with the fear of not being in control. Faith is the tool that allows you to surrender control to the Universe and trust that you are safe and okay in doing so. It is not a tool to be used to duck personal responsibility. Sitting on the couch doing nothing because you have faith that the Universe will provide for you and bring you everything you need is not productive. Action is highly valued and part of the soul's purpose. One of the things your soul is working on in this plane is aligning your actions consciously with your emotional and spiritual desires.

You are learning about your creative power and part of that creative process involves action. You are learning how to take actions that support your goals. So engaging in a permanent state of inaction as a way of "cheating," if you will, is not likely to get you very far. Faith steps in when you have done all you can do and you're ready to give it over to your co-creator, the Universe. Co-creating doesn't mean the Universe creates your desired life for you while you watch television and eat potato chips.

As co-creators it is important to have faith in your creation partner, the Universe. Faith often steps in regarding how something comes into your reality. You may be doing your part to manifest a week in Hawaii, for example, even though you have no idea how you will get the money to pay for the trip or when that will fall into place. The "how" and "when" are your co-creator's department. Worry and doubt about the "how" and "when" will seriously compromise your creation of the goal. However, replacing doubt and worry with faith allows your manifestation process to run much smoother and at times this will affect the timeline of reaching the desired goal. Doubt and worry are akin to sludge in a gear shaft; they slow things down. Faith is like the WD-40. Having faith allows you to create a smoother, more peaceful reality for yourself. Aligning your thoughts, emotions, beliefs, and actions with what you want and then *letting go* is the key to a productive and fruitful creation process. Trying to force things into being or stressing about outcomes is counterproductive to your creative process.

Bringing this subject to a close, let us remind you that you are in control of your personal reality. The creative process you adopt in your life—whether it be one made up of worry, fear, forcing and doubt, or one made up of authentic alignment with your goal and faith—will make a tremendous difference in terms of a peaceful reality or one filled with strain and strife. It's all entirely up to you.

❦ 17 ❦

How to Create Your Reality and Your Role as Co-Creator

LET'S TALK NOW ABOUT this distinction between your role and your co-creator's role. It seems fairly simple on the surface—you are responsible for your thoughts, feelings, beliefs, and actions and the Universe is responsible for the timing and how things come into your life. Looks easy enough on paper, right? Then why is it such a largely misunderstood formula? We'll get into this a little deeper because there are facets to this that need explanation in order for you to understand. First of all, terminology can be tricky for us. We are trying to condense incredibly expansive information into a vocabulary that doesn't always fit. There often aren't words in your language that truly describe what we are talking about. So we have to work with what's available.

When we say your co-creator is the *Universe*, we are running into such a language dilemma. "Universe" is one simple term that allows us to as accurately as possible get the point across, so we use it. But what we are referring to when we say Universe may be your guides helping out (your guides are certainly responsible for guiding some of the "hows" and "whens" in your creative process). Or it may be more of a reference to the universal field of energy full of probability and potential that you are working with. Both are true, but we are trying to simplify our terms for the sake of clarity rather than referring to your co-creator as your guides at times and as the universal force field at other times. That gets confusing. And to be honest, they are distinctions that don't really pertain to our information here—that is, it's not necessary for one to fully grasp or understand such distinctions in order to understand their role as co-creators and the creation process. We only bring it up because some of you reading this may be thinking, *What is this Universe business all about?* Let's just say when we refer to the Universe as your co-creator we are referring to that which goes beyond your control. The "Universe" is where the creation process is out of your hands—whether it be in terms of your guides' role in something or other factors.

That said, let's carry on with our explanation of your co-creative process and responsibilities. First and foremost, your reality is *always* your responsibility. You are always in control of how you choose to perceive things, which in turn creates your reality. For instance, take two people in the exact same scenario. One may be miserable and one may be happy. How can this be, if they are experiencing the same variables in the same situation? It is because they each perceive the situation differently. It can be as simple as waiting for a late bus when it starts to rain. The bus being late is out of your control. The rain is out of your control. But how you respond in this situation and what kind of experience you get out of it is completely up to you. One may get angry and allow this scenario to ruin their mood, even their day, while the person standing right next to them experiencing the same exact variables may choose to let it go and focus on the things in their life they are grateful for, which in turn makes this one little incident not seem like such a big deal in the grand scheme of things. Both individuals are late, both are getting soaked, and one may be at total peace with that while the other is madder than a hornet.

This matter of perception is what creates your reality and you are always in charge of your perception. So it is not accurate to believe your day is awful and miserable because the bus was late and you got wet. That is putting responsibility for your reality on outside forces. The truth is your day is awful and miserable because you chose to perceive it that way. The other person at the bus stop experienced the same exact variables and her day is not awful and miserable, so it doesn't hold up that those variables are responsible for your mood. *You* are responsible for your mood. Ducking personal responsibility is a big thing in your society, so we want to be very clear about this. Whether or not the things showing up in your day are out of your control, you are completely and wholly responsible for how you choose to respond, feel, and perceive those factors. That perception in turn is what creates your reality—not the factors themselves. Blaming outside factors for your reality ducks personal responsibility; as long as you do so, you will always be at the whim of what is going on around you. You will not have any stability in peace and serenity if you continually allow your peace of mind to be dependent upon things going on around you. This understanding of personal responsibility is the first part of understanding and taking conscious control of your creative process.

Next is the matter of "bridging the gap." This goes back to our discussion about different aspects of your self being on different pages. Previously, we explained this in terms of your personal well-being. Now we'd like you to look at it in terms of creating. If you are trying to achieve some particular goal, it is imperative that you align *all* aspects of yourself with that goal. If you are looking for a new job, you need to think, feel, and believe that the job you desire is coming to you. *And* you need to take action toward finding it.

This space of action can often be where a disconnect occurs. Many are very well aware of the importance of aligning their thoughts, feelings, and beliefs with what they want and do so, but then they stop there. The misconception is this: "Okay, I've aligned my thoughts, beliefs, and feelings with what I want. Therefore all my energy is being focused upon attainment of my goal. Now I just sit and wait for it to show up." This is a very common faux pas. Alignment of your self with your goal is crucial and a huge step toward your desired outcome. But you must then take it a step further with action. Action toward your desired goal has powerful energetic effects in drawing your desired outcome into your reality. So if it is a new job you desire, put daily action into that. Ask around, put out resumes, take professional development courses, check the classifieds, keep your eyes on all the sources of job listings.

This action seems rather obvious in the job approach, but in other areas people often forget about the importance of action and rely on the sit-and-wait approach. This sit-and-wait approach may have been effective in some situations in your life and therefore it has been adopted as the useful approach for all situations in your life. This is unfortunately the trap a lot of people fall into. *"If it worked once, it will always work."* There are the rare occasions where a goal is manifested with little or no action. These situations tend to be very few and far between; therefore, we don't encourage this sit-and-wait approach. Find ways to align your doing with what you want. Action is just as much part of the creative process as your thoughts, feelings, and beliefs.

The purpose of aligning your self, in all ways, with your goal is to streamline that creative energy into a creative momentum that in turn brings into your reality the focus of that energy. This isn't really a metaphysical concept but rather one of physics. Please explore this further in terms of the literature available on quantum physics if you wish to have a really in-depth understanding of how this energy attraction works. We are not going to get at this at the level of energy mechanics, so we refer you to explore that on your own if it so interests you.

When you are in alignment with your goals, you are using your powerful creative energy in a conscious way rather than creating haphazard unwanted results in your life through unconscious creation. You see, you are always engaging in this creative process whether you know it or not. Your thoughts, feelings, beliefs, and actions are energy so there is always this creative energetic output. What makes all the difference in the world is whether or not you consciously direct that energy.

That said, let's paint a picture now of what goes beyond your control in terms of creation. This is a multifaceted subject, so people often only see one facet of it and without understanding or knowledge of the other facets involved don't believe that manifestation or the law of attraction works. Here is why. We have just explained your responsibility and role in your own creation process. You are responsible for your perception of events, which will in turn determine to a large extent the quality of your life, and you are responsible for conscious awareness of your thoughts, beliefs, feelings, and actions. That is quite a big chunk to work with! Now this is where people get confused. They become aware of their role in the creative process—which is just one facet—and don't understand when it "doesn't work."

The next facet we wish to share is that of divine timing. That, as we have already explained, is beyond your control. But we remind you, it is a parameter to your creative process that *serves your greatest good*. It is always of service to you, whether you are aware of it or not. Another facet of this process is how things come to you. The mental human brain tries to see through the acquisition of any goal by trying to control how that goal is achieved. This is a fine line between action toward your goal and faith. It is often difficult for the human mind to discern the point where it is beneficial to let go in the process. This is a natural thing—it is part of the brain's job to problem solve and get things done. Therefore it is going to try to bring about its desired outcomes the only way it knows how, without awareness that there is a co-creator involved who is handling this to a large extent.

There is a point in this creative process where you need to understand you are turning it over to your co-creator. Very often you see certain people or places or opportunities as keys to the realization of your goals. You then pursue these options and try to force a partnership, or try to promote yourself to certain people or places because you feel they are the ones who can give you your big break. Then, if it doesn't work out, you may become angry and upset and think you were doing all the right things by taking action toward your goal by approaching people and places you thought would be the key to your goal. What you don't know is the bigger picture in terms of a) your life plan, b) the life plan of others, and c) the greatest good for all concerned. Because you don't know these factors (but your co-creator does!), you have a little help in this area. It is kind of like having tunnel vision when you don't have access to that information. You may see only one or two possible options for fulfilling your goal, where in reality it may be the case where neither of those options serve your best interest overall but there are twenty other potential options you are not even aware of.

This is very much mirrored in the parent-child relationship. A young child is not yet aware of the bigger picture of how things work in their world, but the parent is. Therefore the parent may observe the child trying to accomplish something using only one method (because that is the only method the child is aware of) and know that it's not going to work. Likewise, while the child knows of no other way to reach its goal, the parent clearly sees multiple options and generally steps in and introduces one of these other, more productive methods to the child. The process here is exactly the same as the process regarding your co-creation. Even the reaction is the same: frustration. The child gets frustrated when what he is trying to accomplish won't work, just as adults get very frustrated when they are pursuing options that don't work.

We are not in any way insulting your intelligence by comparing you to a child. As we said in the beginning, you are each remarkable and we are incredibly respectful toward your endeavors. But the parent-child relationship is a useful analogy because you can all understand it. Even if you aren't a parent, you've still been in this relationship with *your* parents or caregivers. The parent-child relationship in its natural form (i.e., not in the dysfunctional form) mirrors your relationship with the Universe. This is why we love the analogy. It is relatable and provides context for much of these confounding concepts.

Okay, so the Universe is taking care of timing and how things show up in your life. The next facet is degree. The degree to which something is accessible to you is often out of your control. Degree refers to "how much." Donald Trump is clearly experiencing wealth to a greater degree than most. This matter of degree can be a grey area because it is also at times under your control. Whether degree falls out of your control depends on the bigger picture and the greater good of all concerned. The degree to which Hitler had power was influenced by the Universe. He was going for total world domination. Without intervention he may have achieved that. We think we would all agree that such an occurrence would not have served the world at large. And so, despite his efforts, and he was fairly well aligned energetically with his goals, the co-creator in this situation influenced how far he was able to go in his dominion, that is the degree to which he had control in the world. This degree of power has often been influenced by the Universe to avoid total world destruction. When, however, it is in one's greatest good to experience their own creative power in determining the degree to which something is experienced in his or her life, there will be no interference. They will have total control of that. So we are putting this matter of degree in the role of the Universe because it does play a role in this factor a lot of times. Just not always.

This is going to be true also for the "how" and "when" factors. There are certainly times when you are in control of how and when something occurs in your life. But at times it is going to be completely out of your control because your desires would not serve the greater good.

You have complete free will and you are the creator of your reality. This sounds contradictory when we get into the notions of the Universe having control over how, when, and the degree to which some things show up in your lives. We want to explain this so it doesn't sound like an infringement upon your creative process or your free will, because it is not. The parameters within which you are creating are not against your will. Nobody's will is ever violated. This may seem contradictory at the conscious level, when you think of instances where you really worked to get something and it didn't come to pass, or instances perhaps where relationships ended that you didn't want to end. This goes back to our explanation of the soul's purpose versus the conscious mind's awareness. Your soul has its intended purposes here. Your conscious mind, mostly unaware of the soul and its agenda, has its own agenda, and very often the agenda of the conscious mind is not in alignment with the soul's agenda. But it's the soul's agenda that serves your greatest good. Again, you can liken the conscious mind to the child, which doesn't yet see the bigger picture of things and the soul to the parent, who does. The child's intentions can be very much in opposition to the parent's intentions in any given situation. The parent usually "wins," however, because they are operating from the perspective of the child's greatest good, which the child can't yet see at his young vantage point. This is essentially what is going on as a deeper part of yourself (your soul) is attempting to get what it came here for and your conscious mind is interpreting the experiences as awful, unfair, or against its will.

If, for example, you set up the intention to meet a certain person and start a business with them and it is very much in both parties' greatest good for that to happen, you might be taking action toward starting your business with others or by yourself and it's not gelling. Yet when you finally meet this one you were intended to partner with, things finally start to fall into place. Your co-creator here had a hand in the "when" of this business taking off because it was working in conjunction with your greatest good and your soul's intended purpose. The conscious self, not knowing this, however, will often become upset and angry and discouraged during that period of things not gelling. You of course always have your free will, though, so you could still choose to not work with the one you were intended to partner with and go in a different direction altogether. The outcomes will be very different and that is fine. There is no "bad" or "wrong" to it. The Universe is merely co-creating with you with a fuller awareness of what serves your greatest good and what your purpose is here. It doesn't mean when such opportunities show up you have to take them.

Another point of clarification we'd like to make is this: When we say the word "intended" as in "the one you were intended to work with," we want to make *very* clear that it is intended by *you*. We are not saying you are intended to do anything in the sense that some outside force is controlling you or setting up your agenda against your will. *You* have set up your agenda and *you* have determined what your intentions are. So if we say you are intended to meet someone, that refers to fulfilling an intention that *you* set while developing your life plan.

It is very important to us that you understand *you* are in control of your life.

This belief of not being in control of one's own life is false, and it's one of the belief systems we'd like to bust the most. Much of the lack of joy and the feelings of hopelessness people have come from feeling like they have no control over their lives. This belief keeps people in a rut where change is difficult. Don't get so caught up in the circumstances—start bringing awareness to *how you handle* the circumstances. It goes back to our friends at the bus stop who are late and wet. Late and wet are just circumstances. How a person handles those circumstances will make all the difference in their world. Something might not be showing up in your world when you think you need it most. You can choose to rage against that or have faith and carry on with joy. Always your choice. It's these choices of yours that determine your reality and your quality of life. People have come to mistakenly believe that it's the circumstances that determine their reality and quality of life.

We are telling you that you are powerful, masterful creators! As such, *you* determine how to steer your life. You determine how to feel about something, what to think about something, what to believe. These are your building blocks of your reality. These are the factors that are going to determine where you go in life and how much you enjoy life. Even those things such as divine timing and how something shows up and to what extent something shows up—those are all factors being endorsed by you, for you. It's just that this is at the soul level which you have consciously disconnected from.

Let's go back now and finish up our explanation of the degree to which something occurs in one's life. As we stated with our example of Hitler, degree of power is often moderated based upon the greatest good of all concerned. If it is not in everyone's best interest to be killed as a result of the detonation of an atom bomb, then one who wishes to attain power for exactly that purpose of detonating a bomb will not be permitted to do so. Power is probably the largest area where degree is moderated by the Universe.

Degree is a funny thing. How much of something one experiences is dependent upon several factors, namely the intended life path of the one creating and the greater good of the whole. Because you are living in a cohesive world community where the actions of one can affect the whole, degree has to be regulated in terms of power, information, even money in some cases. Information, for instance, can be regulated to the degree which people are informed about particular things. If people had information that they would not know how to deal with and thus a large catastrophic outbreak of panic ensued, that would not serve the greatest good. We are not talking about government cover-up stuff here. We are referring to universal truths and principles that are just too complex to be computed by the current human brain. This isn't to say there is scary, fearful information that we are keeping from you—but there is information that can be *interpreted* as fearful or scary or that would topple people's entire belief systems to the point they may become unstable.

There are protective mechanisms in place to ensure mass humanity does not lose its mind. You are privy to the type and amount of information that serves your greatest good. If it's not in your best interest to have your mind blown to the point of insanity, you are not going to receive any type of information that could have that effect. We aren't going to go into this, but we will say this is why there has not been full disclosure and open public interaction regarding extraterrestrial life. What people don't understand they can turn into a threat and act in ways that are not beneficial for all involved. There are a great number of things that, although non-threatening in truth, would be perceived by the human mind as threatening, and therefore the degree to which people have information about such things is moderated.

Okay, so let's recap. Here is a diagram to give a visual breakdown of the roles you and the Universe play in the process of creation:

When you see this visually you can see where the majority of the creative process falls into your control. This is an accurate depiction. You have a tremendous amount of power in determining the course of your life. You already use this power, but it's often unconscious. When the degree to which something is manifested in your life is completely irrelevant, in terms of more or less having a massive effect on others or the detriment to your path, then you are given complete control over that.

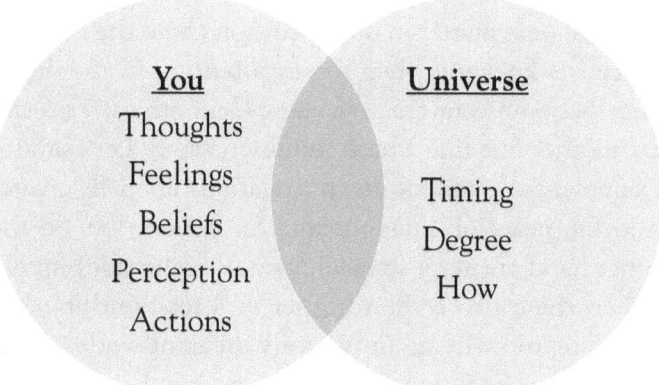

You are really in control of most all of the creative factors—but your co-creators are there to assist when need be due to your current lack of awareness of the bigger picture.

During our process of explanation we realize it may sound like a lot of things are out of your control and this isn't so. You are the primary creator in your life and the driving force behind the manifestation of your reality. Your co-creators are not thwarting your creative process in any way—they merely work on ensuring things unfold in a way that serves the greatest good. This is accomplished by moderating, at times, the "how" and "how much" of your experiences and the timing of your experiences. Again, we want to reiterate an important point. It is not as if these things are being moderated by some force outside of you and against your will. In that sense it is *not* like the parent-child relationship. You are working on your divine life purpose and you have assistance in doing that. Since you have forgotten your plan, you have a little help where your forgetfulness might pull you off track. You are working in concert with your co-creators and you are fully supportive of this at the level of your soul. In fact you *rely* on it at the level of your soul.

The next matter in our discussion about the creation process is knowing when to pay attention to the difference between your creative energy and others. This can be another fine line where confusion arises. Let's say, for example, Sally and Joe are in a relationship. Sally creates a joyful, peaceful, loving reality for herself. Joe, on the other hand creates a stressful, cynical reality for himself. When these two come together in a relationship, they are going to be living in two very different worlds. That is, they may be in the same house, paying the same bills, sharing the same space, but they have different perspectives on life. Because of this, when issues arise, Sally will approach them in a way that demonstrates her knowledge about her creative potential. She will have a positive perspective and align her energy with quick and joyful resolution of the issue. Joe rather, will rail against this "latest set of injustices" and become irritable and angry and resistant.

So if these two need to resolve an issue together, using these two very different and non-complementary strategies, what's going to happen? Chances are they are going to create a new set of issues based upon their disagreement of how to handle/approach the existing issue. When two people are not in resonance with one another energetically, it is very difficult to have a joyful and deeply fulfilling and meaningful relationship. Sally is creating her reality with joy and love and yet she must share space with a partner who is creating a reality of stress and strife. Sally will then become unhappy in this relationship and not feel fulfilled. Joe's reality is not her responsibility, and yet people often lose sight of this and allow another's reality to affect their own in ways that are not joyful for them. Then one becomes confused about where their creative process ends and another's begins.

To be clear—people want so badly for things to work out with partners they may not be well suited for that they take responsibility for their partner's feelings. If your partner is feeling anything, that is his or her experience and his or her responsibility and part of his or her creative process that helps determine the reality that they live in. You are not responsible for another's feelings.

If you are severely mismatched with another and choose to exit the relationship and the other becomes very upset, you may take responsibility for their feelings; you may believe that they are miserable *because of you*. Here is an important truth: You can never create another's reality for them. When you leave a relationship the other person may a) fall to pieces, become bitter and cynical and wall themselves off from people; or b) use the opportunity to grow, move forward and become a happy, vibrant person ready to try love again. Whatever road that person walks, it is not your responsibility. That is their reality to create for themselves.

Remember we said that circumstances don't create your reality but rather how you respond to circumstances is what creates your reality? In this scenario, you leaving the relationship is just a circumstance. How the other person chooses to respond to it has nothing to do with you. So it is not accurate or fair to say one is miserable and lonely because so and so left them years ago. It is never fair or accurate to blame another for the reality someone is living. Likewise, it is equally unfair and inaccurate to believe you are miserable because of someone else and to blame him or her for any unhappiness you feel.

When relationships end, that can be very sad and very difficult. You are likely going to experience intense emotions like sadness, anger, loneliness, and so on. You may indeed feel miserable for a spell. But it is important to own those feelings and that experience. It is not someone else's responsibility that you feel miserable. This is where the line becomes blurry between your creative responsibility and another's. You are interacting with others every day, others who think differently, perceive things differently, hold different beliefs, and feel differently. People all around you are engaged in their own creative process that may look very different from your own.

It is important when people come together and realities clash to know where your personal responsibility begins and ends. Sometimes people are going to do things that upset you. But they are not creating your reality—they are only creating circumstances, and *you* will create your reality based upon what you do with those circumstances.

≈ 18 ≈

The People-Pleasing Epidemic and its Antidote: Self-Love

WE FEEL WE HAVE COVERED quite a bit of territory regarding your creative process. We could truly write an entire book about this alone. As you can see, it is a multifaceted subject with plenty of areas for misinterpretation. But we feel you have a good enough handle on it to move on. As creative beings, you are continually painting your own picture. As such, your life is yours to create and you can make changes anytime you want. This gets tricky. This is where that word "but . . ." comes in and ruins everything! You live in a culture where your training has taught you to care more about pleasing others than yourself. This has become quite a significant hindrance to many people's happiness. People do all manner of things that make them miserable for the sake of others. People remain in relationships with partners they are not in love with for the sake of their partner or children, or what other people will think. People stay in jobs they hate to make others happy or proud of them. People make constant daily sacrifices because they put their own happiness beneath that of others. "*Sure, we can have Chinese food again for dinner!"* (although you hate Chinese food). There are most certainly times for compromise and sacrifice, but you don't need to live your entire life that way. When you continually give over your own desires and joy to another, the message your subconscious mind gets is, "I'm not worthy." If you were worthy, you would honor yourself first and foremost, above all else. Very few of you do this because you have been taught that it is selfish. This is really an unfortunate program that is running in your culture, because it keeps so many of you from loving and honoring your self above all else. That is not selfish; that is acknowledgment of your beautiful divine light!

It feels good to make others feel good. We certainly aren't discouraging you from embracing opportunities to do so. But it should not be at the expense of your self. Imbalance occurs when one is consistently doing more for others than for the self. People are in a constant state of doing for others or trying to please others or catering their own actions and choices to a fear of what others might think. You have lost sight of the most important person in your life—you. You need to fill yourself up before you can truly share with others.

This program of giving to everyone else and having nothing left for the self is causing not only a tremendous amount of stress and unhappiness in people's lives, it is creating illness. If we were to use the term "epidemic" to describe any of your current programs that cause problems, this would be it. It is such an ingrained thing that people aren't even aware of it. And it causes low-level underlying stress and unhappiness that most people don't even consciously detect. But it takes its toll. It takes a toll on one's state of mind, one's joy, and one's health.

Think about what you would love to do right now more than anything in the world. Take a moment and let that come to mind. Okay, so here is this fabulous thing you want to do more than anything else. Go do it. Okay, right there, did you have the word "but" immediately come up when we said, "Go do it"? You likely thought something along these lines, *"I'd love more than anything to do such and such BUT . . ."* But what? Why are you denying yourself? Not enough money? Not enough time? You now know what powerful creators you are—create the money! Create the time! But what about what others will do? What about their needs being met while you're off doing what you want to do? We say, what about *you?* Why aren't you worthy and deserving of being cared for and catered to the way you do others? Why aren't you giving to your self as much as or more than you're giving to others? Ah, here is where the selfish thing kicks in. The belief is that to give more to one's self than others is selfish. Epidemic-level nonsense! That is precisely the belief that prevents so many from fulfilling their dreams and daily joys. If we could extract that one belief from the mind of humanity, your entire world would change. This is not an ego-based *I-am-better-and-more-deserving-than-everyone-else* frame of mind we are suggesting. Quite the contrary. You are more open to others and have more to give when you fully acknowledge your own worth and demonstrate your worth by living for *you.* When you are in a place of balance, you stand in a far better position to be of service to others. But the second you are being of service to others *at the expense of your self,* you are out of balance. You are this most remarkable, radiant, glorious divine being! Own that! Treat yourself as such! You do not treat yourselves the way you would treat God, or

Source. And yet you *are* God, or Source. You have forgotten this truth about yourself and as such you deem yourselves as less worthy than your divine Source. You are not. That's not even close to the truth. You are Source. You are Source incarnate and a supremely powerful being.

The following scenario is one that plays out often in your society. Sally and Mark go to the theater. Mark didn't really want to go, but he knows Sally loves it, so he goes along because it makes her happy. It is fine with Mark to sacrifice three hours of his time doing something that bores him to pieces because it makes him happy to make Sally happy. This is a healthy compromise. Where it becomes imbalanced and unhealthy is if Mark *always* goes along with what Sally wants to do, never speaking up about what he wants and in turn feeling unfulfilled and resentful because they never do anything he wants to do. Sound familiar? This is so common that even if you haven't been in a relationship like this, you likely know others who have. We're sure you've seen it in action. Many people have trouble speaking up for what they want and asking for what they need. You are taught from day one to put your own needs and wants aside to please others. This then manifests in your adult relationships. One person may continually deny his or her own desires simply to please the other. Or perhaps both partners are doing this. When both partners are trying hard to please the other at the expense of their own desires, you have a lot of conversations that go like this:

"What do you want to do?"

"I don't care, it's up to you. What do you want to do?"

"Well, you tell me because really I can do whatever."

"No, you decide. I'm happy doing anything."

Around and around they go. People are afraid to take charge and assert their wishes and desires because they are afraid it will displease the other and then the other will think less of them and then they will feel unloved and then they will feel unworthy. This really all goes back to self-worth. This is the deep-seated root that most people are not even conscious of. People often place their sense of value and worth on how others view them. Therefore, if you please everyone, they will like you. If they like you, then you feel likable and then you feel worthy. When your sense of self is in any way tied to how others view you or what they think of you, then you will be constantly trying to control how others perceive you. You will put their needs first and try to please, putting your own needs in a very secondary role. This is often so subtle that people don't even know they're doing it.

When this happens, your foundation upon which your sense of self worth is built can crumble at any time. It's built on sand, not stone. When your sense of self is built only from your inner validation of your self, completely independent of others and outside factors, it is solid. Nobody can shake it because nobody has the power to. You have not given it to them. There is a huge misconception that to be strong and have a solid sense of self-worth is to be arrogant or bitchy or conceited. This is why people continually denounce their greatness. People don't want to be perceived as egotistical or self-centered.

Loving yourself first and foremost and honoring yourself first and foremost is anything but egotistical and self-centered. It is through genuine, authentic love of self that you may access a genuine, authentic love of others. There is nothing selfish about taking care of yourself and speaking up for what you want. This can be done in a very loving way. Asserting your needs doesn't have to be "bitchy" or "arrogant" or "rude." It can be done with love and in a way that honors all concerned.

We are not talking about putting yourself first at the expense of others. When one continually hurts others and demeans others and invalidates others in the name of "honoring their self," it is in a very ego-based way that has nothing to do with authentic love of the self. In fact, that is another form of dishonoring the self. Loving the self means recognizing and honoring the divine within you. Consequently, that extends to recognizing and honoring the divine in others. To put yourself first with complete disregard and disrespect for others is not an authentic expression of self-love. That is an expression of arrogance stemming from insecurity. Arrogance has nothing to do with an authentic love of the self. Loving your self, in a way that is honoring of the divine, is in essence loving all, because the divine that shines in you is also in everyone else. When you accept this about yourself—when you accept your magnificence—you can't help but acknowledge it in others. That said, you understand when to lovingly assert yourself and you understand the importance of taking care of yourself first and foremost, because from there you can then have something to give to others. Giving to others to somehow validate yourself or fulfill a sense of self-worth is not authentic giving.

An authentic love of self is the recognition of your inherent self-worth, your inherent divine nature. Authentic self-love and self-validation has nothing to do with notions of being better than anyone else. If one's feelings of worth are in any way based upon feeling better than others, that is not authentic self-love, that is the ego. That is the ego's way of trying to compensate for feelings of inadequacy and using others to do so.

Believing that you are less than amazing, less than great, less than wholly and completely worthy, creates this sense of inadequacy. People then try to fill that hole up by pleasing others and creating an outward image worthy of praise. One who does this is looking in the wrong place for a sense of self-worth. It can't be found anywhere outside of the self. Nobody else but you is capable of giving you a sense of worth. This is the misconception—that others can make you feel whole and worthy. If they love you, then you can feel lovable (worthy of love). But if they don't love you, then you feel unlovable (not worthy of love). This is why a large number of people place so much emphasis on being in a relationship. When they are with someone, then they feel loved. If that someone leaves, they don't feel loved and try to quickly replace that feeling by getting into another relationship. Your inherent worth and lovability is not dependent on whether someone else loves you or leaves you. Many people feel that if they are not with someone, then they are no good. This is why people would rather be with someone who they aren't ga-ga over rather than being alone. You all deserve to be ga-ga. If you are finding yourself "settling" in your relationships, you need to ask yourself why. Why is it better to be in a lukewarm relationship than be by yourself? Being with yourself should be awesome because *you're* awesome. Why is this not the case? Get to the root of that and you will discover where you are dependent upon others for your happiness.

Nobody else can "complete you." Nobody else can make you whole. It is your responsibility to feel complete and whole on your own. Then if Mr. or Ms. Right enters the picture, that's icing on the cake. But you don't *need* them to make you feel valued and worthy: You already are.

When you enter into a relationship with a strong sense of self and self-love, you will not be interested in constantly trying to please your partner at the expense of your self. And if they expect you to do this, then they are attempting to use you to feel a sense of love and worth. Two people who are strongly rooted in a sense of self and who love and honor their self will come together without any expectations of the other filling them up in any way. From here, the relationship is free to explore a far deeper and more meaningful experience of love. When you lose sight of yourself in the other person, you are on shaky ground. There is nothing more beautiful than two people who know who they are, joining together to explore love without having any need for their partner to complete them or fill them in any way; they are free to explore love at a different level. They are more likely to experience authentic unconditional love, which is one of the most powerful energies available.

We have spent a lot of time talking about this in reference to romantic relationships because this is where these issues are most evident and problematic. However, the people-pleasing syndrome exists in all relationships. People do this to get friends or to be liked by co-workers. It's happening all the time. One who is engaging in this behavior is likely doing so across the board, not just in romance. If one is looking for others to fill them and give them a sense of worth, they will likely exhibit this in all forms of their relationships.

How many times do you do things that you really don't want to do because there is some program running in you that tells you that you "should"? This is the key indicator to look for—the "shoulds." When you consistently do things you don't enjoy because you think you "should" do them, you are bringing the self out of balance by giving more to others than to the self. People tend to do what they think they should do far more often than doing what they want to do. Honor yourself. Honor your body. Honor your feelings.

Whenever you are faced with this "should" versus "want" scenario, don't go on autopilot. Really examine it. Is it a simple compromise that in the end makes you happy to do for another—like Mark going to the theater with Sally? Or are you completely denying the self for the sake of others or for the sake of what others will think? It's okay to say no. It's okay to say, "Not now." It's okay to say, "Let me think about that and get back to you." There is such a fear of hurting others' feelings or of being perceived as rude, that people often don't speak up for themselves. You can be so busy worrying about the feelings or needs of others that you deny your own. Eventually this leads to anger and resentment, because you become mad that you feel someone is walking all over you or that you are not fulfilled in the relationship. Anger and resentment are two leading causes of illness in the body. Harboring those energies over time most often leads to physical illness or complications. When you are true to yourself, you have no need to harbor anger or resentment. Those energies won't establish in you when you are honoring your self in all ways. You are not responsible for other people's feelings and happiness and likewise they are not responsible for yours. It is safe for you to stand in your greatness. You can be true to yourself while still being kind and respectful to others. Let's segue this into this area of being kind to others, because this is where a lot of confusion arises. You have mis-defined the term "kind" to mean telling others what they want to hear. You believe that to tell the truth when it is something another won't like hearing is unkind. This is false.

For example, you are on a bus and the person sitting next to you won't stop chatting to you; you really need to make a phone call to your children to let them know you will be home late. You may feel that to tell the person you need a moment is rude and unkind. That is not unkind, that is being true to yourself. Here is the true difference between kind and unkind:

Kind: "I'm sorry, I need a moment to make a phone call. I really need to check in on my kids."

Unkind: "Could you shut the hell up already? I need to make a call!"

Telling this person you need them to stop talking is not unkind. *How* you tell them will be an expression of either kindness or unkindness.

Here is another scenario. A friend is not respectful of your boundaries. This friend wants a lot more out of your friendship than you do, although you have already expressed that you are only willing to give so much time to the relationship. This friend calls and/or texts consistently and wants to get together on a regular basis. If this friend is in your space more than you are comfortable with, you can kindly explain to her that you need a little space. Own your own feelings. Being unkind is saying, "You are a royal pain in the ass; would you just leave me alone!" Telling her you need space and kindly reinforcing your boundaries is not unkind, it is honoring yourself.

Now, the friend may not like it and may choose to take offense. When you take responsibility for that and believe that you were unkind to her because you told her something that she chose to be upset about, you are taking responsibility for her reaction and her feelings. You can always be true to yourself in kind and loving ways. If another's response is to get upset, that does not mean you were unkind to them. But this is where you have mis-defined "kind." You feel that to upset another is unkind. Truthfully, you can't upset another—only they can choose to be upset or not. Please keep in mind their feelings are valid. But they aren't your responsibility. Your responsibility is to be true to yourself and speak up for yourself. You can do so with kindness or with malice. That choice is also your responsibility. But please do not equate another's reaction to your being unkind. If you speak your truth with love and kindness, then that is a true expression of kindness. When you say you were unkind to someone because you told them something that made them mad, you misinterpret the term kindness and you take responsibility for their feelings.

Your friend might go around telling people you were mean to her because you said you didn't want to talk on the phone every day or that you needed space. That's okay, that's her misunderstanding of what is her responsibility and what is yours. If she feels you are responsible for her feelings, that is hers to work out. That truly has nothing to do with you. This is where you need to have a strong sense of self. Many of you can't bear the idea of people thinking you are mean or rude. But when others don't yet understand that you aren't responsible for their feelings, you can kill yourself trying to please them in an effort to avoid judgment.

Taking responsibility for the feelings of others prohibits you from owning your feelings. If you feel you can be responsible for another's experience, then you will likewise believe that others are responsible for your experience. This is not so. Others are responsible for the way they present information to you. As previously demonstrated, they can do that in a way that is kind or not so kind. Even if they speak to you in a way that is unkind and hurts your feelings, those are still *your* feelings and *your* choice to experience feeling hurt and taking their words personally. This isn't to say people shouldn't make an effort to be kind to one another. It is incredibly beneficial to embrace the energies of kindness and compassion. These energies are far more healing than their counterparts. When you feel another has hurt you, try to be aware of the distinction between your experience versus their experience. That is a distinction that often gets overlooked.

People constantly come together to help one another with their lessons and life plan. If someone is stirring your emotional pot, then they have come into your life to help you. Friends come in all sorts of guises. Your worst enemies are truly friends at heart. Anyone who helps you gain insight, awareness, or healing of the self is a gift. Learning to take personal responsibility for your experiences and ceasing the blame game is a gigantic leap on your path of self-realization. A person cannot truly demonstrate self-realization as long as they are blaming others.

This can be a very touchy subject and very controversial. It can be incredibly difficult for some to accept that they are responsible for their emotions. When violent crimes occur, it almost sounds callous to human ears to say the victim is responsible for his or her feelings and should not blame the perpetrator. This type of scenario gets a little deeper than the issue of responsibility.

This goes back to the agenda of the soul and the ways in which it chooses to gain expansion. While in this physical realm it seems to you incredibly absurd if not altogether unbelievable that a soul would willingly allow a vicious crime to be part of its experience. But the soul knows it is eternal and indestructible. There is no worry of death there. And the soul (which is you) is most interested in maximizing its learning opportunities while in the physical plane. The mere fact that you live in a plane where violence exists means there are valuable lessons to be gained through that experience. If that were not the case, violence would not exist. If there is nothing for anybody to learn from a particular experience, it would not be available. Things do not exist in the Universe arbitrarily. Everything in existence serves a purpose. There is not a single thing that you experience that is against your soul's will. The soul only engages in experiences that it agrees to.

At times, for some, that will be the experience of being the victim of a violent crime. This happens to be one of the many choices for growth in this physical plane. The experience of being a victim of a violent crime does not end when the crime is over. The one who has endured such a traumatic event continues to experience all manner of emotions related to the experience. People do not walk away from violent crimes going, "Okay, that was unpleasant, but it's over now. Time to move on." No, people carry that experience and all that it unfolds within them for years. Although it seems unreasonable to the conscious mind, there are so many valuable opportunities for one's expansion through such an experience. The aftermath leads to any number of potential growth opportunities. The soul knows that it is not truly going to be harmed through any experience, even the experience of murder, so it looks at everything more in terms of learning potential.

Imagine being an actor in a play. You get into character and go onstage and engage in these relationships with your fellow cast mates. Perhaps your character even gets killed. But then the curtain falls and you walk off stage and get out of your character and you are yourself again, not harmed at all. This is a perfect analogy for what is going on with your soul. It comes into this physical life and engages in all the experiences that will help it achieve its goals and grow, and then it exits stage left and goes back home and reads the reviews. Obviously, your life is more involved than a play, given the depth of physical, mental, spiritual, and emotional experiences you have, but it is essentially the same concept. You come, you learn, you go back home. The soul has incarnated innumerable times and experiences a vast array of both pleasant and unpleasant experiences. And yet here you are, sitting here reading this book. Obviously past traumas did not "kill" you and completely debilitate you. Because here you are. You are once again in a physical body, having a whole new set of experiences.

We don't recommend you go around telling people they chose to be victimized. The soul agreeing to such an experience is a profound spiritual truth and not one that is easily embraced. People need to come to it on their own in their own way. People who have endured violent crimes should not be told that it was merely a growth experience for the soul and to get over it. The unfolding process of trauma recovery is very real and offers a tremendous amount of growth opportunity. To gain those growth opportunities, a person must be allowed to walk that path. They should not be expected to simply "get over it." We are certainly not mitigating anyone's experience of trauma by saying the soul allowed the experience to happen. The effects of trauma are very real and must be worked through to find healing.

Trauma is a prime opportunity for the soul's growth and evolution. From the vantage point of the spirit realm, where you do your life planning prior to an incarnation, the soul sees an opportunity for a traumatic event and thinks, "Oh, look at that wonderful opportunity for expansion! There are all kinds of opportunities in that experience, let's do that!" However, once you have incarnated and you no longer identify with the soul or its agenda but rather with the conscious mind and its ability to feel pain, this seems ludicrous and unjust. There are those who will never in their current physical lifetime accept this truth because it is just too painful.

The nature of the conscious mind is to balk at the experiences that it finds unpleasant and painful. The conscious self has a very difficult time accepting that a part of you allowed such experiences into your reality. This matter of traumatic events is perhaps the most difficult area in which to assume personal responsibility. A person who is violently attacked must be very brave and very self-aware to accept the truth that the soul willingly entered into that situation. In such a scenario the only valid method of perception to the conscious mind is blame—blaming the perpetrator for the pain inflicted. Blame, anger, hatred, this is all part of the process and we are not suggesting one shouldn't have such feelings. We merely want to present you with the bigger picture of what is going on here so you can know the spiritual truth of such situations. That doesn't mean victims of crime won't still have to work through emotions of anger and blame. However, the process can be expedited with an understanding of the soul's agreement to experience such scenarios.

When a traumatic event occurs and it benefits the growth of the soul, the perpetrator was actually playing a role to help serve the growth of that soul. That is why blame is not truly an accurate response. It is a very natural human response and that is okay. You're having a human experience so those feelings are of course valid. Spiritually speaking, however, the perception of blame may not be accurate. That is, it's not exactly an accurate perception that the perpetrator is responsible for the miserable experience one endures through such an event. The soul does not engage in *any* experience without permission. So, as difficult as it is to hear, in any traumatic event the souls involved have agreed to be a part of that. There was not one single victim of the Holocaust who didn't agree—at the soul level—to have that experience. This is very difficult information to process, we know. It is not meant to be discouraging, but rather very liberating. The true reality of things is there are no victims. Souls come to the earth plane to have all manner of experience, both pleasant and unpleasant, and the soul is always honored in such a process. All experiences a soul has, it has given permission for. People are coming together and playing out roles for one another so everybody can get the intended lessons they came here for. In the grand scheme of things there are not truly victims and perpetrators; these are roles that people are playing for the sake of expansion.

Personal responsibility is important to recognize on both sides of the coin. We have discussed the importance of taking personal responsibility for your emotions, your reactions, and your behavior. It is also equally important to recognize where someone else's responsibility lies. It is a common tendency to "take on" others' issues. When someone is very critical or judgmental toward you, there is often a tendency to internalize that rather than recognizing that the person is exhibiting such behavior due to his or her own distorted perceptions and/or beliefs. That has nothing to do with you. This area of judgment is especially difficult because of that external self-worth system that is established in your society. People are very fearful of being judged and therefore take it personally when they are. Judgmental behavior is a person's expression of not yet recognizing his or her own divine self—it has nothing to do with you. When you try to please others to avoid this judgment, you deny your own self-radiance. It can be a difficult thing to take full responsibility for the self and only the self. This has not really been modeled very well for you so it is not a system that you are used to.

How often have you gone to an event with a friend or partner and enjoyed the event very much but worried about whether your friend was having a good time? Perhaps instead of fully immersing yourself in enjoyment, you allowed yourself to worry about whether or not your friend was having a good time. You are not responsible for your friend's experience. And yet you are taught to be hyper aware of everyone else, even at the expense of yourself. This example is classic of taking responsibility for someone else. There is a distinction between being mindful of another's feelings and taking responsibility for them. That distinction is very blurry and unclear to most people.

The people who throw parties and can't relax and enjoy their guests because they are so worried about everything being perfect so that everyone will be happy is another classic example of taking responsibility for another's experience. You can focus on what *you* can do to ensure you are creating a pleasant and enjoyable atmosphere, but then it's best to let it go. Do your best and let it go. You are not responsible for another's experience, another's perceptions, or another's feelings.

People so often forget their own greatness. In your training to please others and take responsibility for others, you have become accustomed to looking always outside of the self—admiring others for their greatness. Inside of you is the greatest gift of all. Housed in your being is the divine essence of the Source from which all is created. That is incredibly powerful. You denounce this awesome greatness in you, and this might be the closest thing to "sin" there is. People are afraid to embrace and shine their light. They fear it may appear arrogant or righteous or prideful. There is a tremendous difference between embracing your divine essence and boasting it. One who has authentically aligned with their divine nature has no need to make others aware of it. One who is seeking admiration and approval from others through "spiritual flaunting" is still misguided in his or her interpretation of what it is to be truly expressing alignment with Source.

When one truly aligns with their divine nature and lives in awareness of their divine light, they naturally exude a peaceful, humble attitude. They need no outside validation or confirmation about their worth. They know who they are and they rest comfortably in that awareness, with no need to convince others of their spiritual understandings. One who rests in his or her greatness is not interested in telling others how great they are. They don't need that kind of attention or approval to feel good. Likewise, one who has a full understanding of their divine greatness knows well that that greatness dwells in all. They will realize that every face they meet is an expression of Source. The one who remembers their truth does not believe it is their truth alone. They understand that the divine dwells in all and therefore you are all connected. Like the light that shines through a prism, throwing off many different fractals of light, the source is the same. You are each unique expressions of Source, experiencing in your own way, exploring your own unique path. There are various expressions of Source, no one greater than the other, from the beggar to the priest to the shaman. You all dwell in this divine essence. The only difference is some know it and embrace it and others do not. But that is okay too. You can't have expectations for others to be where they are not. It is unfair to expect one to experience that which he or she is not ready for. There is a divine purpose behind every path. When one embraces that realization, what follows is a sense of freedom, lightness, and joy.

Be free in your knowledge of self—of who you are and how amazing you are. Be true to the divine essence within you. It is the "real you." The real you is not the identity you have created based upon fear, needs for approval, needs for love and acceptance, needs to feel worthy. That isn't who you are. Who you are is spectacularly glorious and without need for any of the above. You don't need it because you already have it. You are inherently worthy, loved, and accepted. Beginning with you and ending with you is the all of the all. The glorious divine Source made manifest. "Seek and ye shall receive" is good advice indeed. Stop seeking outside of the self, however, and seek from within that divine essence that dwells within you. That is who you are. Because you are already whole and perfect, there is not a whole lot you have to do to embrace this truth. You just need to stop denying it. You need to let go of the yardsticks by which you compare yourself to others and measure your worth. Money, status, looks, job—these are not determinants of your worth in any way shape or form. They have become areas in which you have lost yourself.

There are many areas in one's life where they find their identity outside of the self. One who works out at the gym a lot may form an identity based on that. One who works as the CEO of a company may base their identity on that. Likewise, you create identities for others based upon such things. You very quickly and easily label and categorize other people and allow those labels to form their identity to you. These identities are how you then relate to one another. It is a very diminishing way to view one another and it greatly diminishes your interactions.

For instance, if you have labeled and categorized someone as a "jock," you will then transfer to them all of the attributes that you associate with "jocks." This does not allow you then to perceive other qualities and characteristics that you believe are lacking in "jocks." You diminish a person by putting them in a box with a label. You do this to yourself as well. You identify with your lifestyle, your family, your job. In these identities it is easy to lose sight of the divine essence, which you are. When you put yourself and others into little boxes, you completely lose yourself. You lose touch with your true essence, which has nothing to do with those identities. They are not who you are, they are part of what you are experiencing. There is big difference between thinking, "I am currently experiencing the life of a soccer mom" and, "I *am* a soccer mom." When you believe that is all you are—somebody's mother, somebody's wife, somebody's employee—you deny the much greater reality of who you are. There is nothing wrong with being a jock or a CEO or a soccer mom. All are completely valid paths! But be mindful of thinking you *are* those things. Be mindful of the labels and identities. They may be accurate *to a point* and they may describe what you *do*, but in terms of who you are, those are very limiting labels.

This is why you have such idol worship in your culture. You see someone very rich or very famous and you worship them. They are put on these pedestals because that identity of rich and famous is very appealing and people want that identify for themselves. If your society did not identify a person by what they do or what they have, this idol worship would not exist. It would not matter. But because people have forgotten who they are, their inherent divine worth and greatness, they look to others as superior or better than for having a "neater" identity. You want what they have because you forget that you already have everything that matters. It is very sad how identified with thin, fat, rich, poor, successful, unsuccessful, and so on society is. People, forgetting their own worth and splendor, feel as though others are better than them or that they are better than others. All the while, you are each the face of God walking around every day. You are this radiant, glorious, magnificent being and you have forgotten. You feel bad about yourselves, you feel insecure, you feel not good enough, all the while this spectacular divine light exists in you. Who you are is truly awesome. If you could fully glimpse it in its purity without the filters of your self-judgment, you would be amazed. Who you are is so far removed from the ways you define and determine who you are. You relate to one another based upon your identities, not based upon the fact that you are all God in equal measure.

These identities create a hierarchy system where the secretary feels intimidated by the CEO, the churchgoer feels inferior to the priest yet superior to the non-churchgoers. You feel "less than" in the presence of certain people and you may feel "better than" in the presence of certain people. All of this keeps your focus from the truth—the reality that you are all GREAT. There is no one better than you. That is not possible. How can God be better than itself? We use the term "God" here because it makes the point we are trying to make. It is equally fair to use the term "Source" or whatever term you feel comfortable using to address the divine in all of you. Again, God, Allah, Source, they are all labels. They are different ways to reference the same thing. We are not concerned with what term you call this Source. You can call it Garfield, for all we care. What we do want to impress upon you is the importance of recognizing that Source as part of your being. This is what matters to us. That you begin to see yourself as worthy, whole, divine, and beautiful—*regardless* of what your situation is. You do not have to fit into certain parameters or earn certain labels to earn this feeling of being whole, perfect, and divine. You already are.

The reason this is so difficult for people to accept is because again, there are labels associated with being "divine." People can't believe that one who steals or harms others is divine. What you have to remember is that you are each divine and having an experience in a physical realm where things that seem to contradict your definitions of divinity exist. You are each beautiful divine seekers, having a human experience and all that goes along with that—anger, rage, jealousy, sadness, hatred, love, violence, and compassion. The divine Source is within all of you—it is you. This is the consciousness from which all things are created. One does not have to be fully "enlightened" or kind, loving, and compassionate to be considered divine. Divinity is not selective, it is not earned. It is the birthright of all.

When this truth is embraced and people begin relating to one another at this level of shared divinity, your world will be a much different place. So long as you relate to one another based on identities, or based upon expressions of forgetfulness of who you are, there will be strife and discomfort in your relationships and interactions. Just because one has lost touch with his or her divine nature and behaves in such a way that conveys this forgetfulness does not mean they are not worthy of love and kindness. The very basic nature of your being is divine. You are not separate from your divine Source, and you are not separate from anything else. You are Source and there is no need to view yourself as anything less. Be you. Be beautiful. Be you to the full. You are amazing and we bow in honor to the divinity in you.

∼ 19 ∼

Conclusion: Parting Words

WE FEEL IT IS TIME to conclude our dialogue now. We have spoken with you about numerous subjects, all of which we hope will serve to expand your awareness of who you are and why you are here. You are full of limitless potential and we hope we have helped to bring you to that realization. Enjoy yourselves and have a good time! Love yourselves and love each other. Bridging the gap between the known and unknown, helping you to gain a deeper understanding of yourselves as multifaceted and multidimensional beings—these are goals we hope we have accomplished. We are very proud of you and of the positive change taking place on your planet. You are incredible. Be strong in your self, knowing always that the divine dwells within you.

The breadth and scope of your potential is really quite vast. You must only come to be aware of this and believe in yourself to tap into that. Surrendering to your greatness, with loving humility, is quite possibly the greatest gift you can give yourself and others. When you realize how beautiful, how capable, and how talented you are, you will feel inspired to share your gifts with the world. If you haven't already, we gently urge you to begin a loving process of shedding your skin so that you may step fully into the radiant divine light that you are. There are limitless possibilities for you to spread your light, lend a hand, and help one another.

Before we go, we'd like to mention one more thing. There is nothing in this world as important as your relationship to your self. That relationship is the foundation upon which all else grows. When your relationship with your self is strong, loving, and healthy, you will in turn engage in strong, loving, and healthy relationships with everything around you. Nobody else gets to determine how you feel about yourself. Only you get to decide that. You are completely in charge of your life and your feelings about your life. Nobody else can tell you who you are. They may certainly try, but only you get to decide whether you give value to that input or not. There is nobody else who gets to determine how you feel about yourself, only you. People may project their own self-judgments and criticisms onto you, but only you can decide not to buy into that.

There is so much more we could share with you; perhaps at a later date we will. But for now we feel enough information has been presented to chew on for a while. We love you and we bless you with gratitude and joy. May you know the light that you are and may you shine it brightly forth in all you do. Peace, love, and happiness to you all.

About the Author

Heather Wallace is an intuitive and serves as a translator—one who communicates with teachers in the non-physical realms and records and shares their messages for the purpose of helping people align with their authentic, divine self. Heather's driving goal in all endeavors is to help people realize how amazing and beautiful they are. A former special education teacher, Heather now devotes her time to writing and teaching yoga and dance. She lives in Asheville, NC.

www.ingramcontent.com/pod-product-compliance
Lightning Source LLC
Chambersburg PA
CBHW022101160426
43198CB00008B/307